THE IMPORTANCE
OF BEING CIVIL

THE IMPORTANCE
OF BEING CIVIL

The Struggle for
Political Decency

JOHN A. HALL

PRINCETON UNIVERSITY PRESS

Princeton and Oxford

press.princeton.edu

Jacket illustration: *Handshake* by Jake Nelson from the Noun Project.

Library of Congress Cataloging-in-Publication Data
Hall, John A., 1949–
The importance of being civil : the struggle for political decency / John A. Hall.
pages cm
Includes bibliographical references and index.
ISBN 978-0-691-15326-1 (hardcover : alk. paper)   1. Social ethics.   2. Civil
society.   I. Title.
HM665.H35 2013
303.3'72—dc23   2012036315

British Library Cataloging-in-Publication Data is available

This book has been composed in Garamond Premier Pro

Printed on acid-free paper. ∞

Printed in the United States of America

1 3 5 7 9 10 8 6 4 2

CONTENTS

ACKNOWLEDGMENTS

Several friends kindly offered detailed comments on this book, so sincere thanks go to Frank Trentmann, Siniša Malešević, Peter Bang, Geoff Crawford, Francesco Duina, Ralph Schroeder, Chuck Lindholm, and Lilli Riga. A different sort of debt—and a huge one—is owed to the Nordea Foundation: the peaceful and beautiful housing it provided during a sabbatical year made it possible to write this book. An early version of chapter 5 appeared in the *Journal of Classical Sociology* (2011); some parts of chapter 8 first saw the light of day as "A View of Death: On Communism, Ancient and Modern," in *Theory and Society* 27(4) (1998), and are used here with kind permission from Springer Science and Business Media. Princeton University Press has been superb, and I thank Cathy Slovensky and Peter Dougherty, the most brilliant of copyeditors and publishers, respectively. I have been wholly dependent on the excellent research assistance of Kalyani Thurairajah.

THE IMPORTANCE OF BEING CIVIL

INTRODUCTION

Any book praising civility is likely to encounter this sort of criticism:

> There is something peculiarly unsatisfying about cases with which no decent-minded reader could disagree ... [speaking] up for trust, loyalty, teamwork, dialogue, pluralism, an acceptance of difference and a sensitivity to others ... is not the most world-shaking of moral standpoints. It is hard to see it competing with Machiavelli's *The Prince* or Nietzsche's *Genealogy of Morals* for sheer shock value. Not many works loudly proclaim the virtues of suspicion, disloyalty, uniformity and rampant egoism.[1]

Such criticism can be justified, but it does not apply to this book. A touch of aggression on this point serves the interests of clarity. Civility is not sugary froth but an ideal of visceral importance. Clear claims can be made about it. For one thing, it is possible to specify a condition that is poorly understood, to explain both why it is desirable and why alternatives to it tend to be repulsive. Differently put, analysis of civility will allow us to properly appreciate our better

[1] T. Eagleton, "On Meaning Well," *Times Literary Supplement*, April 10, 2012.

selves, thereby setting up a prescriptive ideal toward which we should aim. For another, "importance" has sociological as well as moral content: civil behavior has powerful and measurable consequences on identity, and these lie behind social decencies. This too can be put differently—by insisting that the normative thrust of the argument is neither vapid nor effete but wholly practical. This is not to say that the ideal is always embraced. Some are misled by the attractions of alternatives; others exhibit sheer folly, often as the result of the love of power. All of this is to say that the analysis here is hard rather than sloppy, as is neatly demonstrated by the praise it bestows on *The Prince*.

The simplest of observations can get us under way: human beings are endlessly imaginative and endlessly silly, with life being at once totally marvelous and utterly absurd. One response to this diversity of condition is the call for civility. An initial reason for the respect it shows toward the varied desires and goals of humanity lies in the realization that it is well-nigh impossible and certainly dangerous to impose any complete set of moral standards in modern circumstances. This does *not* entail absolute denial of all universal moral standards. How could it given that the ideal of civility considers the agreement to differ to have universal status! But a mild relativism does lie at the back of the ideal, an insistence that *few* rules of morality are really grounded. Civility accordingly has an ironic flavor that distinguishes it from those versions of liberalism that insist on severe uniformity, and this despite considerable overlap in philosophical assumptions. The fact that manners, polish, self-command, and calm are then properly seen as elements within civility might suggest an endorsement of the cold and distant behavior of an English butler, not least given the portrayal by Anthony Hopkins of one such figure in the film version of Kazuo Ishiguro's novel *The Remains of the Day*. It would be a mistake to make such a link. Remember the last of George Washington's "Rules of Civility and Decent Behaviour in Company and Conversation": "Labour to keep alive in your Breast that Little Spark of Celestial fire Called Conscience." Jane Austen makes a similar point:

> Mr Elliot was rational, discreet, polished, but he was not open. There was never any burst of feeling, any warmth of indignation or delight, at the evil or good of others. This, to Anne, was a decided imperfection.... She prized the frank, the open-hearted, the eager character beyond all others. Warmth and enthusiasm did captivate her still. She felt that she could so much more depend upon the sincerity of those who sometimes looked or said a careless thing, than of those whose presence of mind never varied, whose tongue never slipped.
> Mr Elliot was too generally agreeable.[2]

Civility does not stand in the way of truth and moral development but is rather a precondition for them. Nor is it the case that civility is tied in some essentialist way to the class-bound eighteenth-century world in which it first reached something of an apogee. On the contrary, civility

[2] J. Austen, *Persuasion* ([1818] New York: Random House, 1984), 116.

is important because it allows disagreement to take place without violence and regularizes conflict so that it can be productive.

But civility is not—or, rather, not just—a "sour grapes" philosophy arguing the negative case that we must put up with a rather undesirable situation since no better way forward can be detected. There is everything to be said in this context for remembering a dictum of Oscar Wilde: "Man is least himself when he talks in his own person. Give him a mask, and he will tell you the truth."[3] Respect for privacy is called for so that there will be room for human beings to experiment with their lives, to try on different masks so that they can, with luck and perseverance, develop their own selves and take responsibility for them. This is a wholly positive case for individuation, made with unrivaled power by Wilde's superb "The Soul of Man under Socialism."[4] And there can be enjoyment as well as despair when observing the antics of mankind. Indeed, such antics can be valued as sources of innovation, the seeds from which social development might spring.

This initial characterization should be taken merely as an orienting device for all that follows. A good deal of light will be cast on the nature of civility by describing the concerns of its enemies, by those who respond to diversity in different ways. But it would be irritating to have too much of an im-

---

[3] O. Wilde, "The Critic as Artist," in *Oscar Wilde: The Major Works* ([1891] Oxford: Oxford University Press, 1989), 282.
[4] O. Wilde, "The Soul of Man under Socialism," in *De Profundis and Other Writings* ([1891] London: Penguin, 1973).

manent critique, presuming that the character of civility can be established merely by specifying its antitheses. So it is worth emphasizing that the intent is to offer a positive specification of civility; this explains the ordering—positive before negative—of the two parts of this book. But before turning to the general argument, three preliminary points must be made so as to highlight the character of the treatment of civility offered here.

Naturally enough, many wonder about the state of civility in contemporary circumstances. The intolerance of current political debate has led some to note a decline in civility, together with calls for its revival.[5] In contrast, a superb ethnography has suggested that civil practices are arising in a wholly unplanned manner in the United States, in arenas where African Americans confront the public sphere.[6] Sociologists have added to this the interesting discovery that incivility in public places is far from being the preserve of lower social strata, however defined.[7] Such studies matter a great deal, and comments in these areas will be made. But this book goes beyond measuring the state of play of civility to confront something more basic, at least in the eyes of the author, a European all too aware of the historical record. The best way to underline my first preliminary point is to note that Norbert Elias's celebrated claim that there is a civi-

[5] S. L. Carter, *Civility: Manners, Morals and the Etiquette of Democracy* (New York: Basic Books, 1998).
[6] E. Anderson, *The Cosmopolitan Canopy: Race and Civility in Everyday Life* (New York: W. W. Norton, 2011).
[7] P. Smith, T. L. Phillips, and R. D. King, *Incivility: The Rude Stranger in Everyday Life* (Cambridge: Cambridge University Press, 2010).

lizing process is wholly wrong.[8] For Elias's book was published in 1939, only to be followed in the next six years in
Europe and in Asia by war, ethnic cleansing, and mass murder. So the first appearance of civil society was followed by
savagery, which makes it necessary to analyze an initial creation and then to examine a later reconstruction—in light
of an understanding of the forces that opposed it. Accordingly, civility is not something cast in stone, not the necessary unfolding of the logic of social evolution; rather, it
comes and goes in waves and needs care and attention if it is
to be maintained. It is necessary to struggle to establish decency in political life, and that condition cannot be secured
without continual effort. This seems to me such a basic matter that it explains why this book pays so much attention to
the vagaries of European history. Of course, the horrors of
the historical record do not make the ideal of civility any
less desirable; after all, one can value what is fragile. But it
does suggest modesty, above all, recognition of the certain
fact that civility does not warm the blood like wine.[9] Bluntly,

[8] N. Elias, *The Civilizing Process*, 2 vols. (Oxford: Blackwell, 1969 and 1982).
This point has been forcefully made by S. Malešević and K. Ryan, "The Disfig-
ured Ontology of Figurational Sociology: Norbert Elias and the Question of
Violence," *Critical Sociology* 38 (2012). The authors note the steady increase in
deaths from organized violence over time (7.8 million for the sixteenth and sev-
enteenth centuries, but 19 million for the nineteenth century and 111 million
for the twentieth century), and add to this the discomforting fact that the educated have played a major role in the perpetuation of horror. On this later point,
see M. Lange, *Educations in Ethnic Violence: Identity, Educational Bubbles, and
Resource Mobilization* (Cambridge: Cambridge University Press, 2012).
[9] J. M. Cuddihy describes civility in these terms: "It is not the warm, dense close-
ness of 'real' solidarity. It is 'formal' solidarity. In a regime of civility, everybody
doesn't love everybody. Everybody doesn't even respect everybody. Everybody
'shows respect for' everybody. Social equality, like legal equality, is 'formal,' not

civility stands opposed to romanticism. If this limits its general emotional appeal, it most certainly increases its merits in my eyes. This first point leads directly to the second. Analyses of civility have told us a great deal about "microbehavior," from associational life to the character of relations in public, and this approach will be extended in the rest of this book. Nonetheless, the life chances of civility have very often depended on "macroforces." A comment must be made immediately about nationalism. In a fundamental sense nationalism stands opposed to the very base of civility: it seeks unity, in contrast to civility's desire to manage diversity.[10] But nationalism is a labile force that can take different forms. Absolute correspondence between state and nation may not be a universal requirement if arrangements can be made for several nations to live under the same political roof. So questions about civility matter enormously within the theory and practice of nationalism. And attention does not focus solely on nationalism but rather on the macroforces with which it interacts—above all, war, capitalism, and revolution.

'real.' In public, everyone is thus equal; yet, one may be private in public, and keep one's 'real' feelings to oneself, till one gets home. True, this is not 'solidarity forever'; it is solidarity ad interim, for the time being." *No Offense: Civil Religion and Protestant Taste* (New York: Seabury Press, 1978), 210. This is accurate, but I differ from this brilliant author, one of whose texts is discussed in chapter 4, in warmly embracing what he dislikes. It is worth noting further that J. Alexander, *The Civil Sphere* (Oxford: Oxford University Press, 2006) offers a warmer and more romantic view of civility, but one in which hope triumphs over experience, prescription over realistic sociology.

[10] A. Wimmer, *Nationalist Exclusion and Ethnic Conflicts: Shadows of Modernity* (Cambridge: Cambridge University Press, 2002).

It may be helpful to make a personal comment here. I write as a sociologist, believing that my discipline has gone through three stages. The first of these had at its center the seminal contributions of Karl Marx, Émile Durkheim, and Max Weber, the holy trinity of the sociologists. A second stage was essentially formalist, obsessed with the creation of concepts and methods at the expense of a sense of reality, with "grand theory" and "abstracted empiricism," as the American social critic C. Wright Mills put it.[11] That period has by no means ended, but it now runs alongside a third period, led above all by comparative historical sociologists who are rethinking everything from nationalism to the nature of "society," from gender to geopolitics, and from revolution to class. This book is firmly within this third period, and, indeed, seeks to add to it. Civility is important sociologically for the two reasons already mentioned. On the one hand, it adds an essential descriptive component that allows us to understand what it is about our societies that is desirable, thereby establishing a crucial prescriptive ideal. On the other hand, civil behavior has important consequences; softness changes the character of social action, thereby making the norm practicable—which is not to say that it is always recognized and adopted. And beyond this stands an expansion of the sociological canon. The three founding figures already mentioned were, in different senses, anticapitalist thinkers, as is made clear in *Capitalism and Modern Social Theory*, the famous treatment of their thought by

---

[11] C. W. Mills, *The Sociological Imagination* (New York: Oxford University Press, 1959). This second period looks set to run forever, reinforced both by endless imports from Paris's Left Bank and by the marvels of modern methodology.

Anthony Giddens.[12] But to consider modern social theory
in this manner is akin to playing Hamlet without the prince.
One needs to know why certain social theorists endorsed
and admired capitalism—not least, it can be added, because
the theorists in question were wholly and powerfully sociological in character—if one is to make sense of the response
that resulted. This is one reason for devoting an entire chapter to Adam Smith, with reflections on several other thinkers designed to further expand the canon of sociology.

The third point concerns the general cultural context
necessary for a proper understanding of the nature of civility. Without further ado, let it be said that there are three
main currents, three main ideological options, within the
modern world. To say that reality is a little more complex
than any simple theory is immeasurably dull. Theories become powerful not from inclusion but from exclusion. Just
as utilitarianism gained enormous power from saying that
only pleasure and pain existed, so too is the claim here meant
to be strong: there are three and *only* three ideological options available to us. Of course, elements of the three positions can and have been joined; equally, all have merit,
though some may seem more attractive than others. One
benefit of this trinitarian view is to make us skeptical of the
imperialist claims of modern economics, so keen to stress
the dominant position of economics within social science,
not least as that discipline fails, as we shall see, to understand the most high-powered theory, that of Adam Smith,

[12] A. Giddens, *Capitalism and Modern Social Theory: An Analysis of the Writings
of Marx, Durkheim and Max Weber* (Cambridge: Cambridge University Press,
1971).

within its own tradition. A still greater benefit is to understand the sentiments that lie at the back of alternatives to civility.

The first version comprises liberal politics, capitalist economic organization, and the modes of thought of rational science. Within this world there is, of course, great variation. For one thing, liberal politics may or may not be democratic; for another, capitalism may be more or less restrained by the polities within which it operates. But if we leave these important matters aside, some general points can be made. Crucially, this is *a* world, not *the* world: it is less the end of ideology than a very particular ideology. It is spare and limited, suggesting that there are benefits to not filling out the world completely. Above all, the respect for genuine knowledge entails a certain moral emptiness. It is at this point that civility makes its contribution by adding to such basic liberal ideas and practices its insistence on an agreement to differ within specified limits. Interestingly, the stance in question is clearly present in the eighteenth century in Montesquieu. Any human being can feel pain, he insisted, thereby ruling slavery out of court and suggesting a politics designed to minimize fear; beyond this, relativism rules, as in the relations between men and women—complex, variable, and often ridiculous for Montesquieu, and certainly not the proper subject of any universal edict.[13]

The second version can neatly be introduced by noting that its greatest thinker, Rousseau, began his career with a long attack on Montesquieu, who had rejected the tradition

[13] J. Shklar, *Montesquieu* (Oxford: Oxford University Press, 1987).

of civic virtue in favor of an acceptance of the complexities
and confusions of the modern world. Rousseau was horrified
by this attitude: moral complexity and division can only
bring psychic discomfort. There is a certain oddity here. The
apostle of individualism bases everything he says on the weakness of human beings, their need for social support—and,
quite possibly, religious meaning as well. We cannot manage
by ourselves, as unrestricted individualism will inevitably lead
to chaos and unhappiness. These sentiments led Rousseau to
admire Sparta, and he accordingly agreed with Xenophon
that—to use the nice expression of Adam Ferguson—virtue
should be the business of the state.[14] This is the tradition of
belonging. This theme gained enormous prominence after
the eighteenth century, which is not surprising given the dis-
ruptive social changes brought about by the transformation
to industrial society. Marx's thought, for example, stresses the
need to remove splitting, to restore unity to mankind: an end
to alienation means that human beings can again be seen as
creators in many different spheres rather than dull specialists
in one. There is, of course, a measure of confidence in the individual in Marx that is wholly lacking in Durkheim, who
was so deeply influenced by Rousseau: the sociologist believed he had shown that individuals bereft of social support
were prone to kill themselves.

The concern with belonging is at the back of much social
theory. Communitarianism descends from the tradition of
civic virtue rather than from the tradition of civil society.
There is a "malaise" to modernity, as the Canadian social

[14] A. Ferguson, *An Essay on the History of Civil Society*, 4th ed., rev. and corrected
([1773] Hants, UK: Farnborough, 1969), 267.

theorist Charles Taylor puts it, such that happiness can only be found through fraternity, through being embedded within a rich cultural tradition, very often of a nation and a religion.[15] Understanding all this can also enable cognitive development within sociology, past the point at which it has for so long been stuck, by placing its central presuppositions within the larger cultural context.

The view of man in much of the first tradition, especially in Montesquieu and in the Scottish moralists, is naturalistic. Human beings are driven by passions of varied character, a view disliked by the second tradition, which sees us in more elevated terms, as spiritual beings. The third tradition, exemplified by Nietzsche and Freud, differs from both. It stresses the instinctual desire for domination. It has no time at all for the elevated moral tone of communitarianism, regarding this as a dreadful escape from truly knowing ourselves. But the naturalism it describes differs from that of the first tradition.[16] The passions are seen, so to speak, in the

[15] C. Taylor, *The Malaise of Modernity* (Toronto: Anansi, 1991).

[16] One way of making the point is to cite Hume's reaction to the philosophical discovery that little made sense in the world:

> The *intense* view of these manifold contradictions and imperfections in human reason has so wrought upon me, and heated my brain, that I am ready to reject all belief and reasoning, and can look upon no opinion even as more probable or likely than another. Where am I, or what? From what causes do I derive my existence, and to what condition shall I return? Whose favour shall I court, and whose anger must I dread? What beings surround me? And on whom have I any influence, or who have any influence on me? I am confounded with all these questions, and begin to fancy myself in the most deplorable condition imaginable, inviron'd with the deepest darkness, and utterly depriv'd of the use of every member and faculty.

light of Darwin. Smith's benign view of human behavior is one based on jealousy, of working hard to attain what others have. But there is also envy. When my neighbor has a Mercedes, which makes me feel inferior with my Honda Accord, one option is not to work harder but to steal out in the dead of night to scratch my neighbor's car. "He hath a daily beauty in his life that makes me ugly," muses Iago when hoping for the death of Cassio.[17] Of course, envy is but a perverted element of the more general desire for power. And one should stress perversion. This third tradition makes much of the certain fact that our instincts are devious and half-hidden from us, placing rationality at something of a discount. But the crucial, deeply worrying contribution of this tradition remains its awareness that the exercise of power can be pleasurable.

It is easy to see how these elements can interact. Replacing the emptiness of the first option seems to have worked best when blood was joined to belonging. This combination

---

Most fortunately it happens, that since reason is incapable of dispelling these clouds, nature herself suffices to that purpose, and cures me of this philosophical melancholy and delirium, either by relaxing this bent of mind, or by some avocation, and lively impression of my senses, which obliterate all these chimeras. I dine, I play a game of backgammon, I converse, and am merry with my friends; and when after three or four hour's amusement, I wou'd return to these speculations, they appear so cold, and strain'd and ridiculous, that I cannot find in my heart to enter into them any farther. (D. Hume, *A Treatise on Human Nature* [(1739 and 1740) London: Routledge and Kegan Paul, 1985], 316; emphasis in original)

The ease, even self-satisfaction, of this position is miles away from the ruthless and haunted world of Nietzsche.

[17] William Shakespeare, *Othello*, act 5, scene 1.

of the two traditions proved to be terribly dangerous and all-too-attractive to a large number of intellectuals. Maynard Keynes realized this and sought to save the world of civility when it was faced with power systems blessed with ideological fervor.[18] It is largely because of this that my own preference is for the first tradition, despite the cogent arguments of both of the other positions. In negative terms, one can insist that it is the least bad alternative. But a more positive eighteenth note is possible. We are or ought to be grown up. Down with the enthusiasm seeking warmth and unity! For Kantian reasons, let us be masters of our own souls!

The book has been carefully constructed. The first half offers a composite definition of civility, stressing both ideas and the structures that support them; the second half seeks illumination by turning to those who dislike civility, and who propose alternatives to it. Both parts move systematically from the micro- to the macrolevel. Naturally enough, the division between these two parts is not watertight; consideration of the endorsers often brings in comments about the opponents, and vice versa. For example, nationalism is considered from different angles in chapters 3, 4, and 10. Further, the emphasis is on analytic clarity rather than on chronology. So the creation and reconstruction of civility is analyzed in the first and third chapters, long before an account is offered in chapter 10 of its destruction in the middle of the last century.

Chapter 1 offers an account of the social origins of civility in the course of an argument distinguishing civility from

[18] R. Skidelsky, *John Maynard Keynes*, 3 vols. (London: Macmillan, 1983, 1992, 2000).

civil society—or, rather, insisting that civility must be included in the definition of civil society if that concept is to carry the weight placed upon it. Attention then turns in chapter 2 to the nature of capitalism by recalling in the simplest terms the sophisticated sociology of Adam Smith, so often ignored and so very far removed from contemporary economic theory. The claim of the chapter is simple: namely, that competitive consumption is a support to civility. Chapter 3 claims that the way states behave, in civil or authoritarian ways, affects our social identities, and in the process says something about the reconstruction of civility. It is here that the key sociological content of civility is spelled out. Chapter 4 recognizes that the rules of civility can vary, making them at times very hard to understand, let alone to accept. A contrast is drawn between the differential abilities of the European Union and the United States to "let in" immigrants so as to create one out of many—an area in which the contemporary United States far outperforms Europe. Chapter 5 considers the great contribution of Raymond Aron to the understanding of civil behavior between states. The second part of the book begins with three related chapters considering in turn the dangers of authenticity, the alienation of many modern intellectuals, and the excessive moral demands of communism—or, differently put, attention is given to an alternative generic ideal, an explanation of the agents who created it, and an analysis of its most important practical instantiation in a social world in which virtue most certainly became the business of the state.[19] The final two

---

[19] I am well aware that the other revolution of the twentieth century, fascism, was as much an enemy of civility; the fact that it is not considered here does not

chapters present a negative view of the state, thereby standing as counterpoint to the positive argument put forward in
chapter 3. Chapter 9 shows how the state can undermine
civility by destroying cooperative relations in society. The
last chapter considers the toxic relations between empires,
nations, and states in the period between 1875 and 1945
that brought disaster to the modern world. The conclusion
considers two especially serious limitations to the tradition
under analysis, but against these is set the marvelous growth
of civility in the non-European world.

---

derive from any bias, more that it was, in comparison to communism, so short-
lived and so militaristic.

PART ONE

A COMPOSITE DEFINITION

CHAPTER 1

Agreeing to Differ

For about a quarter century "civil society" has had about it an air of excitement. This is not surprising, for the concept has been taken as a banner by those wishing to be free in Eastern Europe, Latin America, and, most recently, in North Africa, and it has been further invoked by Marxist thinkers in the West who seek a nonstatist theory of the Left.[1] Still, there has always been vagueness as to exactly what the notion implied. This chapter provides the clarity that is needed. The argument is simple: "civil society" only "makes sense" when it contains a heavy dose of civility. It may be helpful to offer a complete definition of civil society immediately: it is a form of societal self-organization that allows for cooperation with the state while permitting individuation. A great deal hangs on "individuation."

The most obvious alternative to my definition conceptualizes civil society simply as societal self-organization. A moment's thought makes it quite obvious that this will not do. To begin with, militancy guarantees nothing nice. Weimar Germany was torn apart by the fanatical enthusiasm of

[1] J. Cohen and A. Arato, *Civil Society and Political Theory* (Cambridge, MA: MIT Press, 1992).

Nazi and communist groups who were keen to fight it out on the streets.[2] Equally, the exceedingly solidaristic self-organization of mafiosi, whether in Sicily or in contemporary Moscow, quite obviously has the capacity for destroying basic societal decencies. Sheer intellectual provincialism makes many forget that settled existence depends on the rule of law being guaranteed by effective state power. The intellectual roots of this blindness derive from nineteenth-century England. A thinker such as Herbert Spencer could imagine a moral world based wholly on contracts between individuals, and this bias worked its way into modern thought as a whole via neoclassical economics. Interestingly, if curiously, this view was taken over wholesale by Karl Marx. The "withering away of the state" that Marx expected under socialism characterizes the general point most evocatively. The fact that the twentieth century has seen viciously effective states that ignored the rule of law provided experience that seemed to underwrite this antistatist ethic. But if despotism is a danger, so too is anarchy. Those who talk of the desirability of curtailing the powers of the state, whether in nineteenth-century England or in twentieth-century United States, overgeneralize on the basis of the pacific consensus that marks their social worlds. This is provincial because it takes no account of bastard feudalism or of Beirut in its worst days, and thereby fails to provide safeguards against further savageries of the type that they represent. Social forces that destroy a liberal state or prevent it from operating efficiently do not contribute to a civil society; that term

[2] S. Berman, "Civil Society and the Collapse of the Weimar Republic," *World Politics* 49, no. 3 (April 1997): 401–29.

should be reserved for social self-organization that cooperates with a responsible and responsive state.

It is just as important to stress that the manner in which members of the organizations mentioned are controlled is far removed from any connotation of the word "civil." The classic instance to bear in mind is that of tribal self-organization,[3] which not only destroys organized states but also controls human beings to such a degree as to rule out any possibility of individual self-determination and moral growth. The all-powerful tyranny that closed groups can exert over every aspect of daily life, from clothing to the choice of marriage partner to the details of belief, is antithetical to any concept of civil society. Positively put, a civil society is one in which individuals have the chance of at least trying to create their own selves. This means that the membership of social groups must be voluntary and overlapping, for it is in the complex interstices of social life that individualism often resides. Furthermore, there is likely to be an elective affinity between civil society and fashion: for all the silly pretensions to which the latter can be prone, it remains the area in which many can experiment with and try on new conceptions of their selves.

These considerations have by now entered into general understanding. But there is something behind antipathy to such "caging" that has not been understood to anything like the same extent.[4] It can be stated very straightforwardly be-

[3] E. A. Gellner, *Conditions of Liberty: Civil Society and Its Rivals* (London: Allen Lane, 1994).
[4] The notion of caging runs throughout the greatest philosophical history of our time: Michael Mann's *The Sources of Social Power*, 4 vols. (Cambridge: Cam-

fore turning to its theoretical exemplar and an account of its genealogy. Civility is based on recognition of difference and diversity. Caging is dreadful in large part because it presumes that there is one road to truth in all matters. Varied attitudes can be involved here. Some welcome diversity enthusiastically, while others put up with it with resignation. A still more sophisticated attitude is that of those who think that a good deal of truth can be discovered but who are reluctant to force-feed human beings into accepting every detail of a morality. This was the position, for example, of the narrator of Marcel Proust's *À la recherche du temps perdu*: seeing a young boy about to waste years, as he had wasted them himself, along the false trails of "society" and art, Marcel refuses to intervene—on the grounds that moral learning can only take place through making one's own mistakes. A key analytic point derives from this. That type of holistic liberalism represented by Durkheim, in which socialization is all-encompassing and all-effective, is not at all civil. A civil society will allow the individual room to experiment, doing so most of the time from a position of mild relativism—that is, one that doubts the presence of a single set of universal rules about every aspect of behavior. Relativism of this sort needs to be distinguished from total or blanket relativism. To say that the recognition of difference is *shared* and the decision to live together with diversity is *mutual* is to note a background consensus, an agreement to differ, that enables civil society to flourish. The consensus in question should,

bridge University Press, 1986, 1993, 2012, 2013). Volume titles are: vol. 1, *A History of Power from the Beginning to A.D. 1760*; vol. 2, *The Rise of Classes and Nation-States, 1760–1914*; vol. 3, *Global Empires and Revolution, 1890–1945*; and vol. 4, *Globalizations, 1945–2011*.

of course, be minimal, including, most obviously, respect for the rule of law, attention to empirical evidence, and abhorrence of violence, while its characteristic attitude will be that of ironic and affectionate amusement at the foibles of humanity within the resulting settled world. All this can be expressed more bluntly: the diversity that is acceptable to civil society is that within a particular world with its own boundaries.

There are several thinkers who both theorize and exemplify civility. To my mind, the greatest is Montesquieu, whose worldview is brilliantly laid before us in his early philosophical novel, *Les lettres persanes*. The skepticism of the book is at times open and bluntly stated. The story of the troglodytes prefigures the distaste that Montesquieu had for the political theory of the ancient world. The disciplined and unitary world of civic virtue demanded too much of us, and it was—as he would show in the book he wrote next, *The Considerations on the Grandeur and Decadence of the Romans*—far too militaristic. In contrast, Montesquieu has sympathy for wealth rather than virtue, and famously asserted later in *The Spirit of the Laws* that the interests might limit the passions, that moneymaking (to make use of Samuel Johnson's expression) might be less dangerous than the pursuit of political power.[5] But the witty iconoclasm resulting from Persians observing our customs, and from our observing their own, is much more subtle. Montesquieu can be seen time and again almost throwing his hands up, with varied mixtures of delight and despair,

[5] A. O. Hirschman, *The Passions and the Interests: Political Arguments for Capitalism before Its Triumph* (Princeton: Princeton University Press, 1977) is acknowledged as the classic account of this tradition.

when considering how we should live. Virtually everything
that we take for granted—food, religion, love and sex, much
of politics, art—is the result of custom, and is thereby
wholly bereft of philosophical grounding. He goes to an extreme in one instance: the only wholly happy relationship in
the book is, it is not always realized, an incestuous one between a brother and sister, Apheridon and Astarte. More
typical, however, is his wry amusement. Women and men
deceive each other, for sure, but the fact that women have a
measure of negative resisting power is far from bad, as Rica,
the more sympathetic and open-minded of the two Persians,
stresses:

> If [the Asians] in their turn argue that Europeans can-
> not be happy with women who are unfaithful to them,
> the answer is that this faithfulness, which they make
> so much of, does not prevent them feeling the indiffer-
> ence which always ensues when passion is satisfied;
> that our wives are too exclusively ours; that being so
> firmly in possession leaves us nothing to desire, or to
> fear; that a certain amount of fickleness is like salt,
> which adds flavour and prevents decay.[6]

Uzbek, the dominant Persian character, makes the same
point.[7] He admits, without any sense of what this means,
that the very possession of the women in his harem has destroyed his desire for them—and the story of the novel

[6] Montesquieu, *Persian Letters*, trans. C. J. Betts ([1721] London: Penguin,
1973), 92.
[7] Ibid., 46.

shows his inability to relinquish control, even though it makes him miserable. Montesquieu had attended salons run by aristocratic women, and it is surely from this background that he gained his occasionally bemused admiration for the independence of women. Fashion might be a little ridiculous, but it allows for moral experiment, for the trying on of different personalities.

The extensive relativism stressed by Montesquieu, the insistence that we really do not have any basis for much of what we believe, has decided and absolute limits. It is again Rica who makes the point most strikingly, in a letter to Uzbek.

> I can tell you that I knew nothing about women until I came here. I have learnt more about them in a month than I should have done in thirty years inside a seraglio. With us everyone's character is uniformly the same, because they are forced. People do not seem what they are, but what they are obliged to be. Because of this enslavement of heart and mind, nothing is heard but the voice of fear, which has only one language, instead of nature, which expresses itself so diversely and appears in so many different forms. Dissimulation, which among us is so widely practiced and essential an art, is unknown here. Everything is said, everything can be seen, and everything heard. The heart is exhibited as openly as the face. In conduct, in virtue, and even in vice, there is always something spontaneous to be perceived.[8]

[8] Ibid., 129–30.

So there *is* a voice of nature, a true grounding for some universal values. *The Persian Letters* makes it clear that slavery is wrong, as is despotism, whether political or religious: both speak the language of fear—and fear is something universal. We can go a little further. The famous letter on suicide notes the cruelty of being punished twice: first for the misery that some people find in existence and then with the social opprobrium of having the suicide's body dragged through the street. This says something about civility. Montesquieu is its best representative because he is aware of horror and had indeed witnessed torture in his early career in Bordeaux. Some eighteenth-century proponents of civility speak of polish and refinement, and so sound a little prissy. Montesquieu is harder: civility is a necessary virtue to help us negotiate a world of pain. That is why he places so much emphasis on knowledge and, above all, on toleration, itself almost a synonym for civility.

It is important at this point, as we move from the character of civility toward an account of its genealogy, to warn against a misconception. Gore Vidal once suggested that the deepest meaning of *Creation*, his magnificent novel about the origins of the world religions and ethics, was that agrarian civilizations before the advent of the great monotheistic creeds were the most tolerant in the history of mankind. There is some justification for this view. On the one hand, the logistics of agrarian civilization meant that they had no capacity to penetrate let alone to police the thoughts of the tribes and peasant communities over which they ruled. On the other hand, monotheism brought in its train the potential for—and, with Christianity once Constantine had converted, the enthusiastic and vicious practice of—intolerance, even though the principle of universal salvation envisaged and allowed the incorporation of all human beings into society for the first time. Nonetheless, the classical agrarian civilizations were not civil societies. Civility has everything to do with the modern world, in which differences conflict with one another rather than being ignored because people live in social silos that do not interact. What matters is the agreement to tolerate, albeit within clear limits, so that it becomes possible to live in peace.

The origins of toleration of this sort lie within Europe. Perhaps its deepest roots result from the way in which the removal of the centralized authority of Rome placed power in several sets of hands.[9] What is most striking in comparative perspective is the separation between ideological and political power. This separation has its origins in Jesus's injunction to deliver to Caesar what was Caesar's, but to give to God what was God's—a remark that amounts to saying that Christianity's concern was with spiritual salvation rather than political order. Christianity later refused to provide ideological justification for Rome, and it found thereafter that it could survive and prosper without the benefit of an imperial polity. Once it realized that it could not itself create a theocracy, fear of concentration of power in the hands of a secular emperor led the church to encourage kings whom they made more than primus inter pares by ritual anointing and the singing of the *Laudes regiae*. If those policies were conscious, very different activities by the church may have

[9] J. A. Hall, *Powers and Liberties: The Causes and Consequences of the Rise of the West* (Oxford: Basil Blackwell, 1985).

done as much to encourage state formation in Europe. The church's greed for land seems to account for the breaking up of obligations toward one's extended kinship network; if the way in which this resulted in a family pattern responsive to Malthusian pressures is well known, the manner in which its atomization of society made for easier state-building may be quite as important.[10] Nonetheless, it would be a mistake to imagine that royal power became unfettered as the result of these two forces. Rather, state-building took place within a field of preexisting social forces. Kings were faced with feudal nobilities whose property rights were firmly established, as were those of the church. In these circumstances kings sought to enhance their powers by granting autonomy to towns; these became islands in the feudal sea in which new ideas and social practices could develop. So here was an acephalous world in which liberties were both widespread and firmly codified in a legal system that privileged corporate rights.

This vesting of power into separate bodies might have led to a static society in which different sources of power merely blocked any sense of a common enterprise. This did not happen, with European society in consequence gaining a restless dynamism that changed the pattern of world history. A measure of cooperation was initially made possible by the sense of unity provided by Christian norms; shared membership in a civilization certainly helped to revive and deepen economic interaction even within the medieval period. But over time a patterned and interactive division took place. State-society relations within countries became in-

[10] J. Goody, *The Development of the Family and Marriage in Europe* (Cambridge: Cambridge University Press, 1983).

creasingly intense due to the endless competition in war caused by life within a multipolar world of states. The need for monies for war led to the practice of calling assemblies of the realm, that is, of church, nobles, and townsmen, to whom were added representatives of the peasantry in parts of northern Europe.[11] Such assemblies took over tags of canon law—"what touches all must be agreed by all" and "no taxation without representation"—which gave Europe a sense of the rule of law. Of course, the fact that there were several states was of enormous importance. A measure of internal decency was encouraged once it was realized that foul treatment of key social elements might encourage them to move and thereby to enrich rival states, as clearly happened when the Huguenots were expelled from France. The presence of avenues of escape supported both economic and political liberties.

This account is slightly exaggerated. Central and Eastern Europe took a turn away from such diversity in the fifteenth and sixteenth centuries as nobles and kings allied against towns and independent peasantries. In northwestern Europe, in contrast, states remained rule-bound even during the period of absolutist rule. In general, however, multipolar pluralism was sufficiently well entrenched as to rule out the success of any attempt—whether by popes, emperors, or kings—to re-create imperial unity. Nonetheless, it is very important to stress that civil society gained in self-consciousness from the experience of fighting against politico-religious unification drives. It is this background that ex-

[11] G. H. Myers, *Parliaments and Estates in Europe to 1789* (London: Thames and Hudson, 1975).

plains the rise of toleration. Attempts at suppression of the religious diversity created by the Reformation failed because Charles V's imperial pretensions were destroyed by the balance of power politics. The principle of cujus regio, ejus religio, enshrined in 1555 at the Treaty of Augsburg, seemingly allowed for diversity and difference, at least between states. But the principle was not really accepted and internalized, as the brutality of the Thirty Years' War so massively demonstrated. The Westphalian settlement of 1648 is a better marker of development in European attitudes since it went beyond the principle established at Augsburg to the attempt to take religion out of public life altogether, one mechanism toward which end was the insistence that existing religious groups within states should be allowed to worship as they saw fit.

The long religious wars of Europe could not be won by either side, for the forces of pluralism were always sufficient to defeat any drive to political-religious unification. Sustained caesaropapism failed. Facing an endlessly destructive stalemate, an extraordinary shift in attitudes slowly took place: if agreement on detailed matters of belief could neither be reached nor imposed, a background consensus, to tolerate religious difference, was a viable alternative. If toleration was at first merely accepted as a sour grapes philosophy—that is, one imposed by circumstances beyond one's control—it came to be positively valued. In the spirit of Marx, one can say that civility "in itself," in which negative resisting power was great, became civility "for itself"— a world in which the principle of toleration was not just accepted but positively embraced. It is important to emphasize that this development was by no means inevitable, and certainly not the necessary unfolding of the logic of social evolution; rather, it was largely fortuitous, although it is worth noting that stalemate is a factor that has had important effects on other occasions. It is also important to note that the principle of toleration went well beyond religious difference.

A brilliant recent history has demonstrated that liberal attitudes to sexuality were quite as much involved and formed the background of the world described by Montesquieu.[12] Between 1600 and 1800 a revolution occurred that took sexual matters from the public to the private realm—within which there were all sorts of mixed sentiments, sometimes constraining but at other times emancipating.

The initial breakthrough to civilized acceptance of difference in Europe obviously predated the emergence of capitalism, with Montesquieu insisting later that the spirit of toleration then facilitated the triumph of this new economic system—a view interestingly different from Max Weber's celebrated notion that the Protestant ethic helped push economic life forward. But capitalism did have something to do with the establishment of a culture of political civility in England, for soft political rule was not always present there; on the contrary, it was a historical achievement. Seventeenth-century England had been prey to civil war, treason trials, regicide, conspiracy, and the sundering of families. The very sudden move to political stability between 1675 and 1725

[12] F. Dabhoiwala, *The Origins of Sex: A History of the First Sexual Revolution* (New York: Oxford University Press, 2012).

seems to be best explained by such traumatic experience.[13] In a condition of continuing stalemate, in which neither side was capable of outright victory, it suddenly began to make sense, as it had to those divided by religion in early modern Europe, to try to live together—the successful accomplishment of which then fostered a culture of civility. Though this political achievement was genuinely autonomous, it was nonetheless aided by economic factors. For one thing, the stalemate itself resulted from negative resisting power in society being widely spread. For another, the acceptance of party alternation in government was eased by the presence of a growing economy that provided sources of remuneration other than that derived from the possession of power.

Civil society reached an initial apogee in eighteenth-century Britain. Historically, new levels of self-organization were made possible by the spread of periodicals, coffeehouses, and associations, all of which were underwritten by a vibrant commercial society.[14] This is the world of Adam Smith and David Hume, just two of the great theorists of Edinburgh, the Paris of the North, as well as of Edward Gibbon and Edmund Burke. Individualism flourished in this world. The modern novel, which allowed discussion and thought about new types of social identity, attests to this.

[13] J. H. Plumb, *The Growth of Political Stability in England, 1675–1725* (London: Humanities Press, 1967).
[14] N. McKendrick, J. Brewer, and J. H. Plumb, *The Birth of a Consumer Society: The Commercialization of Eighteenth-Century England* (London: Hutchinson, 1983). There is one difficulty with the subtitle of this book: commerce mattered quite as much to the Lowlands of Scotland, as such "North Britons," as Smith and Hume realized.

Political innovation marked the age quite as much as these basic social forces. John Wilkes stands as the exemplar of popular politics, concerned at one and the same time with popular representation and the interests of the English nation. No similar set of developments marked the world outside the Occident. To analyze the social portfolios of a set of different civilizations is almost impossible at all times, and certainly so here. Still, something can be said about the ideas and institutions of three other civilizations. The point of these limited remarks is that of underlining—rather than explaining—the claim made: namely, that civil society did not emerge endogenously outside the Occident.

At the ideational level, little evidence can be found of interest in a shared world within which difference is respected. Islam certainly stands opposed to this. What is most noticeable about this religion is the supreme confidence with which it provides a complete set of injunctions designed to apply to politics as much as to matters of salvation.[15] The great tradition of this religion was not flexible enough to easily adapt itself to different political regimes as was Christianity, let alone keen to allow for toleration. At first sight, the Hindu-Buddhist synthesis of Indian civilization seems the exact opposite of this, essentially tolerant in the relativism of its insistence that there are many ways in which to find salvation. But this position is equally hostile to the notion of civil society. The Western notion depends

---

[15] M. Cook and P. Crone, *Hagarism: The Making of the Islamic World* (Cambridge: Cambridge University Press, 1977); P. Crone, *Medieval Islamic Political Thought* (Edinburgh: Edinburgh University Press, 2005).

on a shared world within which limited differences are accepted; Indian civilization stands in contrast to this for the brute reason that difference is absolute, with even the shadow of an untouchable able to pollute a member of the higher castes. It may well be that Confucianism, whose ethic of politeness superficially resembles the British upper-class insistence that "manners makyth man," stands closest to the Western notion. But that ethic never faced ideological rivals, preferring rather to retreat from power at any moment when its standards were temporarily placed in question. Mannered self-restraint may well be important in Chinese civilization, but, in the last analysis, this was not occasioned by, nor necessary for, the management of ideological difference—let alone as a shell designed to allow human individuation.

There are, of course, myriad, complex, and varied relations between ideologies and institutions, making the following comments about the latter alone especially arbitrary. Still, the extent to which the social patterning of the non-Western civilization stands opposed to civil society is very striking. The certainty and completeness of Islam gave no room for mundane politics; this so weakened states as to occasion an endless cycle in which corruption was always replaced by a new despotism; the fact that this was allied to perpetual, external military threat from tribes ruled out limited, civil politics. The organization of Indian civilization by means of caste made states quite as weak—with the prospects of a short tenure of power again occasioning predation upon, rather than cooperation with, the forces of society. Chinese civilization did depend on a long-lasting state, but the difficulty here was that the coincidence of political and ideological power left no room for societal organizations that were able to balance the state. Of course, in all three civilizations, there was intense social organization. But such organization was either private or directed against the state: social actors faced states that were either short-lived and predatory or long-lasting and cohesive—and tended in any case to be caged by kinship-based organizations. In every case social patterning was far removed from any notion of civil society.

We can leave this account of the character and genealogy of civility by pointing to problems to be addressed as we proceed. The first appearance of civil society was neither complete nor secure. For one thing, the imitation by backward societies within Europe did not encourage civility. If there was an initial link between commerce and liberty, as Adam Smith claimed, the planning of capitalism from above did not sustain it. For another, the behavior of European states in the rest of the world was anything but civil. Remember the slave trade. Additionally, European "liberalism" within empires overseas was characteristically dogmatic and vicious. Most important of all was the attempt to install unitary virtue during the French Revolution. What matters here is not the Terror itself but rather the reaction that it bred—that is, the determination of old regimes to stay in power at all costs. There is everything to be said for taking the French Revolution as a symbol of the moment at which the people enter onto the political stage. Thereafter states needed, at a minimum, to integrate both classes and nations if they were to be stable and successful. Civil society

before the French Revolution had not faced these challenges, which is to say that its sense of propriety and refinement was the creation and property of the few. The tragedy
of European civilization is that political elites that might
have modernized their polities failed to do so. The lesson
these diehards learned from the behavior of the Jacobins
was wrong: they sought to batten down the hatches rather
than to modernize by inclusion. We will see in chapter 3 the
way in which exclusion affected class and nation so as to
cause disaster; the analysis of recovery that follows high-
lights the crucial discovery of the way in which inclusion
moderates political life.

A final reflection forces itself upon us. The twentieth century has seen ideocracies that are opposed to the ideal of
civil society, thereby making it crystal clear that the modern
world has been very far from uniform: there is no single
"modernity." Insofar as this is so, civil society *is* but one option among others, that is, an ideal born in the West that
faces alternatives. This lends a certain measure of schizophrenia to anyone endorsing civil society. On the one hand,
awareness of enemies makes explication and analysis important in an internal sense: it makes it possible to understand
ourselves, so that what we value can be better defended. On
the other hand, recognizing that civil society is a world
among others puts on the agenda the desirability of finding
rational grounds by means of which to choose one world
rather than another. Most defenses of civil society of this
sort ultimately tend to be negative, to stress the failure of
alternatives and the fact that there is some connection between civil society and prosperity. Such defenses have cog-

nitive power but they are unlikely to persuade everyone, not least given those flaws to its pedigree soon to be noted. While not impossible, it is only fair to say that producing transcultural argument on this point is notoriously difficult. In the final analysis, I suspect that civil society can only be defended in Kantian terms, that is, on account of its respect for the individual.

CHAPTER 2

Sympathy and Deception

We have seen that commercial society helped (and continues to help) civility by making the exit from political power bearable given that access to wealth serves as a means to status and comfort other than that of the possession of political power. More important still is the view, present in Montesquieu, that moneymaking is more innocent than the search for power. Maynard Keynes captured this point when commenting on his own social philosophy:

> There are valuable human activities which require the motive of money-making and the environment of private wealth-ownership for their full fruition. Moreover, dangerous human proclivities can be canalised into comparatively harmless channels by the existence of opportunities for money-making and private wealth, which, if they cannot be satisfied in this way, may find their outlet in cruelty, the reckless pursuit of personal power and authority, and other forms of self-aggrandisement. It is better that a man should tyrannise over his bank balance than over his fellow-citizens; and whilst the former is sometimes denounced

as being but a means to the latter, sometimes at least it is an alternative.[1]

Both these points concern the behavior of members of the elite. But much more is involved, as the social theory of Adam Smith so brilliantly reveals. Smith is poorly understood. Sociologists know almost nothing about his work. Contemporary economists are nearly as bad by failing to realize the extent to which his system rests on premises far removed from their own. Smith was a *general* theorist of very great rigor. We will turn to the basic model of commercial society first before considering his view of social development; both these areas contain surprises for anyone imagining Smith to be the proponent of capitalism Chicago-style. But the core of the chapter revolves around his view of the way in which an illusion keeps the mechanism of capitalism working. If balance rather than originality characterizes what follows, compensation is to be found by spending time in Smith's company.[2] The mind

---

[1] J. M. Keynes, *The General Theory of Employment, Interest and Money* ([1936] London: Macmillan for the Royal Economic Society, 1973), 374.

[2] The scholarship on Smith is now exceptionally high-powered. I have relied on D. Winch, *Adam Smith's Politics* (Cambridge: Cambridge University Press, 1978) and *Riches and Poverty: An Intellectual History of Political Economy in Britain, 1750–1834* (Cambridge: Cambridge University Press, 1996); C. Griswold, *Adam Smith and the Virtues of Enlightenment* (Cambridge: Cambridge University Press, 1999); N. Phillipson, *Adam Smith: An Enlightened Life* (New Haven, CT: Yale University Press, 2010); M. L. Frazer, *The Enlightenment of Sympathy: Justice and Moral Sentiments in the Eighteenth Century and Today* (Oxford: Oxford University Press, 2010); R. P. Hanley, *Adam Smith and the Character of Virtue* (Cambridge: Cambridge University Press, 2009); and F. Forman-Barzilai, *Adam Smith and the Circles of Sympathy: Cosmopolitanism and Moral Theory* (Cambridge: Cambridge University Press, 2010).

is boggled when recognizing that perhaps the two greatest forces of the modern world, science and capitalism, were first theorized by two friends, Hume and Smith, living in Edinburgh in the second half of the eighteenth century. They were not always in agreement.

There are two essential presuppositions to Smith's basic model of commercial society. The first is outlined in the celebrated opening passage of *The Wealth of Nations*. Ten men working together, Smith tells us, are capable of producing 48,000 pins in a single day; in contrast, each of those men working alone would only have been able to produce about 20 pins a day. Economic success results from the way in which the division of labor enhances productivity. Adoption of this principle explains why modern society has, in comparison with those of the past, attained a level of universal opulence. But the division of labor will do little good, indeed might be dangerous, unless a second principle is adopted. Human beings have a natural disposition to "truck, barter and exchange," and this must be let loose before the division of labor can bring its benefits to mankind as a whole. It is worth emphasizing that this last expression is carefully chosen. Smith was one of the earliest theorists of comparative advantage, that is, of the theory that all nations can enter a positive sum game by specializing in those products or industries in which they are specially gifted. He saw no reason why the development of poorer nations should enfeeble richer nations in any absolute sense.

On the basis of these two principles, Smith constructs his argument. We can reconstruct his position by spelling out the various steps that stand as intermediaries between and behind the division of labor and the end result of universal opulence. Three steps are of especial importance. First, Smith goes to great lengths to explain exactly why it is that the division of labor so increases productivity. Specialization allows for a division of function, and thus for an increase in dexterity and expertise. In a nutshell, an increase in human capital is the essential ingredient allowing for improvement within commercial society. The last element at work is an increase in machinery, but it is one that should most certainly not be exaggerated. After all, the first steam locomotives were just being invented in the early 1800s. But the economy that Smith is describing is not an industrial one, and it was certainly one without many factories, the pin-making example having misled many at this point. Indeed, the fact that the sources of power did not yet include the regular use of fossil fuel meant that Smith's hopes for economic growth in all probability had a distinct ceiling fixed to them: he believed that wealth could be achieved but was far from envisaging the endlessly growing cornucopia of goodies that industrial capitalist society has been able to provide with marked effectiveness after 1945.[3]

The second step of the argument places the market principle before the division of labor. People will only be moved to divide labor—and to undertake the exercise in productivity just noted—if it is worth their while. The larger the market, the more likely that specialization and opulence will

[3] E. A. Wrigley, *People, Cities and Wealth: The Transformation of Traditional Society* (Oxford: Oxford University Press, 1987) and *Continuity, Chance and Change: The Character of the Industrial Revolution* (Cambridge: Cambridge University Press, 1990).

follow. This principle makes it relevant to emphasize yet again that Smith wants commercial society to be as extensive as possible. His principles make him a resolute foe of protectionism of any sort, which he saw as a tax on the consumer of the worst sort, as it diminished the general welfare of society in order to look after lazy special interests.

Behind the market principle stands, finally, something more basic still: namely, the principle of self-interest. Altruism, love, and benevolence do not, Smith commented, lead us to exchange products with a baker; rather, it is the fact that such exchanges can be mutually satisfying that encourages people to enter the market. At this point, Smith has some resemblance to Bernard Mandeville, whose celebrated poem "The Fable of the Bees" suggested that private vices could lead to public virtues. It is not conscious agency that causes economic development but diffuse and decentered processes. Everyone thinks of their own self-interest, but, almost miraculously, a hidden hand—effectively the laws of supply and demand—ensure that society as a whole benefits. This seems to raise a fundamental problem. If everyone thinks of themselves, how can social cohesion be possible? It can be said immediately that Smith's social theory deals with this problem, as we will soon see, in the most high-powered manner imaginable.

One fundamental reason why Smith so strongly endorsed the commercial society of his time was that it created wealth. The principal tradition of political thought with which he was faced stressed the need to maintain virtue in order for a society to avoid corruption. The survival of Greece and of republican Rome depended on the virtue and, above all, the physical fitness of citizen soldiers, something that classical authors held was likely to be undermined by luxury. Smith helped effect a revolution in human thought by insisting that wealth was more important than virtue. The principal reason for this was absolutely straightforward: classical society had been based on slavery, and this was offensive to the central members of the Scottish Enlightenment. Just as David Hume felt that every human being had the same sensations, so too did Smith believe that a good society should provide a sufficiency for every person. This implicit egalitarianism—which must not be confused with endorsement of the practices of modern democratic processes—is evident throughout *The Wealth of Nations*. Early in the book Smith writes glowingly about the social, economic, and demographic progress in North America, where people have a great deal of control over their lives, and contrasts it in this way with the situation in China:

> China has been long one of the richest, that is, one of the most fertile, best cultivated, most industrious, and most populous countries in the world. It seems, however, to have been long stationary. . . . The poverty of the lower ranks of people in China far surpasses that of the most beggarly nations in Europe. In the neighbourhood of Canton many hundred, it is commonly said, many thousand families have no habitation on the land, but live constantly in little fishing boats upon the rivers and canals. The subsistence which they find there is so scanty that they are eager to fish up the nastiest garbage thrown overboard from any European

ship. Any carrion, the carcase of a dead dog or cat, for example, though half putrid and stinking, is as welcome to them as the most wholesome food to the people of other countries. Marriage is encouraged in China, not by the profitableness of children, but by the liberty of destroying them. In all great towns several are every night exposed in the street, or drowned like puppies in the water.[4]

The tones of disgust are unmistakable.

But it is not just the wealth that commercial society produces that leads Smith to endorse it so strongly. He is impressed with the fact that humans living within the market are far less likely to be corrupt than the mainstream political theory of his time allowed. Intelligence and information are necessary if one is to learn of one's best opportunities. In other words, life in the market encourages independence of mind and judgment. The deference of more traditional societies is seen by Smith to be morally repulsive: it is necessary for an individual to scrape before the powerful as a dog cringes before its master when wanting a bone, hoping that such a display will produce patronage and favor. We shall hear more about the moral improvements brought about by commerce later.

Given the misuse of Smith by academics and politicians, it is worth emphasizing that Smith had, in line with the points already noted, considerable sympathy with labor. In purely economic terms, he favored high wages; this was

[4] A. Smith, *An Inquiry into the Nature and Causes of the Wealth of Nations* ([1776] Oxford: Clarendon Press, 1976), book 1, chapter 8, 89–90.

scarcely surprising given that the engine of commercial society was its human capital. This is not to say that he failed to recognize the fundamental differences between capital and labor: on the contrary, in the bluntest terms he declared that the conflict of interest between them over the social product was inevitable and irremediable. Still, he had many more hostile things to say about merchants, most famously in his declaration that "people of the same trade seldom meet together, even for merriment and diversion, but the conversation ends in a conspiracy against the publick, or in some contrivance to raise prices."[5] Such a sentiment makes it necessary to inquire into both the emergence and the maintenance of commercial society.

The bare bones of Smith's account of the emergence of commercial society are as follows. The collapse of the Roman Empire led to the creation of a militaristic society in which physical power ruled life chances. In these circumstances, it made much more sense to keep one's property in land rather than in trade:

> The man who employs his capital in land, has it more under his view and command, and his fortune is much less liable to accidents than that of the trader, who is obliged frequently to commit it, not only to the winds and the waves, but to the more uncertain elements of human folly and injustice, by giving great credits in distant countries to men, with whose character and situation he can seldom be thoroughly acquainted.[6]

[5] Ibid., book 1, chapter 10, 145.
[6] Ibid., book 3, chapter 1, 377–78.

The lack of security of property diminished the activities of traders in the most obvious way:

> In those unfortunate countries, indeed, where men are continually afraid of the violence of their superiors, they frequently bury and conceal a great part of their stock, in order to have it always at hand to carry with them to some place of safety, in case of their being threatened with any of those disasters to which they consider themselves as at all times exposed.[7]

Still worse, from the point of view of economic improvement, was the fact that feudalism discouraged agricultural development. Smith ruefully tells us that men love to domineer, and that this instinct was well accommodated in the manorial system—with consequent diminution of productive capacity.

If the prevalence of political power was characteristic of nearly all life within the agrarian era, a uniqueness of Europe stood out even during what Smith would certainly have felt to be the Dark Ages. Historical sociology normally shows, in Smith's opinion, that progress takes place first in the country, with towns taking a very secondary role. Europe differed in Smith's view, and in that of later scholars, in having towns that were centers of genuine production.[8] This economic vitality was encouraged by political autonomy. The kings who ruled Europe after the fall of Rome were ex-

---

[7] Ibid., book 2, chapter 1, 285.
[8] M. Finley, "The Ancient City: From Fustel de Coulanges to Max Weber and Beyond," *Comparative Studies in Society and History* 19 (1977).

ceedingly weak in relation to their leading nobles. In order both to raise revenue and to create a balance against their nobilities, they granted charters of autonomy to the towns. Feudalism was a "power system" in which any excess wealth was most rationally invested in retainers—whose military prowess would then allow robbery and the acquisition of territory. But the productive city provided luxuries upon which the aristocracy came to spend their monies. It is this that both Hume and Smith felt undermined feudalism:

> But what all the violence of the feudal institutions could never have effected, the silent and insensible operation of foreign commerce and manufactures gradually brought about. These gradually furnished the great proprietors with something for which they could exchange the whole surplus produce of their lands, and which they could consume themselves without sharing it either with tenants or retainers. All for ourselves, and nothing for other people, seems, in every age of the world, to have been the vile maxim of the masters of mankind. As soon, therefore, as they could find a method of consuming the whole value of their rents themselves, they had no disposition to share them with any other persons. For a pair of diamond buckles, perhaps, or for something as frivolous and useless, they exchanged the maintenance, or what is the same thing, the price of the maintenance of a thousand men for a year, and with it the whole weight and authority which it could give them. The buckles, however, were to be all their own, and no other human

creature was to have any share of them; whereas in the more antient method of expence they must have shared with at least a thousand people. With the judges that were to determine the preference, this difference was perfectly decisive; and thus, for the gratification of the most childish, the meanest and the most sordid of all vanities, they gradually bartered their whole power and authority.[9]

One particular point in this passage needs explication. We have seen that Smith felt that the security of property was a necessary precondition for commercial society. Kings had tried to achieve this, but they had been defeated by the power of their overmighty subjects: what mattered more than conscious plans were the unintended consequences of vanity. Smith's underlining of the point drips with irony:

A revolution of the greatest importance to the publick happiness, was in this manner brought about by two different orders of people, who had not the least intention to serve the publick. To gratify the most childish vanity was the sole motive of the great proprietors. The merchants and artificers, much less ridiculous, acted merely from a view to their own interest, and in pursuit of their own pedlar principle of turning a penny wherever a penny was to be got. Neither of them had either knowledge or foresight of that great

[9] Smith, *Wealth of Nations*, book 3, chapter 4, 418–19.

revolution which the folly of the one, and the industry of the other, was gradually bringing about.[10]

The emergence of commercial society was thus as fortuitous as was the acceptance of toleration, the result of a curious concatenation of circumstances rather than of any sort of historical inevitability, let alone the result of conscious plans by humans.

What is perhaps most striking about Smith's theory is the extent to which it is not economistic in character. One way in which this is so concerns the nature of the causal pattern that Smith identified. Smith certainly felt that a rather restrained state was necessary for the economy to flourish. But behind that political factor stands an economic factor—namely, that these luxuries, produced in cities, undermined the feudal order. But behind that factor stands another political consideration: the parcelization of sovereignty after the fall of Rome that led to cities gaining autonomy in the first place. Thus, the rise of commercial society is seen as a long interaction of political and economic factors, at once autonomous and intertwined. But another point of still greater importance is beginning to become apparent. Smith's ultimate values were liberal: he endorsed commerce in the largest part because it went with liberty, that is, a softer and more regular political system which undermined political arbitrariness. Commercial society was but an effective means toward the end of softer political rule.

[10] Ibid., book 3, chapter 4, 422.

The notion of the restrained state is not as straightforward as it might seem; accordingly, it will need and receive further elucidation in a moment. Before doing so,
however, we will now turn our attention to the core of
Smith's contribution. Analytical clarity can be enhanced
by asking how Smith expected a society so clearly based on
self-interest to hold together. This is what German scholars
called "the Adam Smith problem," the apparent contradiction between the stress on self-interest in *The Wealth of Nations* and the totally different view of human motivation in
his earlier *The Theory of Moral Sentiments*. Are the two
books complementary, or are we dealing here with mere intellectual schizophrenia?

The Theory of Moral Sentiments is a measured and confi-
dent book in which Smith was profoundly convinced that
the society of his time was bringing about civilization.

That we often derive sorrow from the sorrow of others,
is a matter of fact too obvious to require any instances
to prove it; for this sentiment, like all the other original passions of human nature, is by no means confined
to the virtuous and humane, though they perhaps may
feel it with the most exquisite sensibility. The greatest
ruffian, the most hardened violator of the laws of society, is not altogether without it.... By the imagination
we place ourselves in his situation, we conceive ourselves enduring all the same torments, we enter as it
were into his body, and become in some measure the
same person with him.... His agonies ... begin at last

to affect us, and we then tremble and shudder at the thought of what he feels.[11]

Human beings are seen here largely in naturalistic terms, as subject to passions or drives beyond their conscious control. But the passions in question are genial rather than bestial. This account of the nature of sympathy lies behind the description of the way in which human beings form moral judgments. Smith is a classical representative of what has usefully been dubbed the emotivist theory of ethics, which claims that we approve of certain types of conduct because they make us feel contented. What this leads to in *The Theory of Moral Sentiments* is the argument that propriety is valued most highly in social life. It is clear that we do not ourselves like to feel disturbed by excess of any sort on the part of others and we appreciate joy rather than pain, as well as the familiar rather than the novel. Crucially, our empathetic capacities are such that we realize that loud and aggressive behavior on our part would cause our fellow citizens similar discomfort. Accordingly, we judge our own behavior from the point of view of an abstract "universal spectator": anything that might disturb the peace of mind of this mythical figure is avoided. It is important to stress that Smith's account goes a little further than this to allow for punishment.[12] We feel for the person who has been injured by bad behavior and allow punishment to appease his resentment.

[11] Smith, *The Theory of Moral Sentiments* ([1759] Oxford: Oxford University Press, 1982), part 1, section 1, chapter 1, 9.
[12] Frazer, *Enlightenment of Sympathy*, chapter 6.

Crucially, in this there is an implicit egalitarianism at work here, and one that goes well beyond Hume, whose moral principles are based largely on concerns for public utility. "When a single man is injured, or destroyed, we demand the punishment of the wrong that has been done to him," Smith argued, "not so much from a concern for the general interest of society, as from a concern for that very individual who has been injured."[13]

This account of the psychology of human beings can easily be named. The celebrated American sociologist David Riesman argued in *The Lonely Crowd* that the American character was changing—and implicitly deteriorating— as the "inner-directed" individualism of the early Puritan founders was being replaced by the "other-directedness" of a consumerist mass society.[14] Smith is an exponent of what Riesman so disliked: propriety, order, and good sense distinctively rule over any expressions of radical individualism. This is intellectually remarkable. Many theorists presume that the rise of capitalism was related to the rise of individualism. This was not so for its foremost theorist. The fundamental human motivation for Smith is the desire to be approved and admired. This can be particularly clearly seen in the passages in which he analyzes rank—that is, class. It is natural, he maintains, for humans to admire and to seek to reach the same level as those above them.

This leads him to distance himself further from the prin-

[13] Smith, *Theory of Moral Sentiments*, part 2, section 2, chapter 3, 90.
[14] D. Riesman, with N. Glazer and R. Denney, *The Lonely Crowd: A Study of the Changing American Character* (New Haven: Yale University Press, 1950).

ciple of utility at the core of Hume's thought. The way in which he does so is—given the interest we know the later *The Wealth of Nations* shows in opulence—positively startling. Smith asks himself if there is any real basis to the widespread belief that the possession of an increasing number of goods actually increases happiness. His answer is a resounding negative:

> In the languor of disease and the weariness of old age, the pleasures of the vain and empty distinctions of greatness disappear.... Power and riches appear then to be, what they are, enormous and operose machines contrived to produce a few trifling conveniences to the body, consisting of springs the most nice and delicate, which must be kept in order with the most anxious attention, and which in spite of all our care are ready every moment to burst into pieces, and to crush in their ruins their unfortunate possessor. They are immense fabrics, which it requires the labour of a life to raise, which threaten every moment to overwhelm the person that dwells in them, and which while they stand, though they may save him from some smaller inconveniences, can protect him from none of the severer inclemencies of the season. They keep off the summer shower, not the winter storm, but leave him always as much, and sometimes more exposed than before, to anxiety, to fear, and to sorrow; to diseases, to danger, and to death.[15]

[15] Smith, *Theory of Moral Sentiments*, part 4, chapter 1, 182–83.

This might seem a conclusive argument against all kinds of economic striving. But it was not for Smith. The fact that the human imagination is wrong in believing that riches bring happiness is profoundly to be welcomed:

> It is well that nature imposes upon us in this manner. It is this deception which rouses and keeps in continual motion the industry of mankind. It is this which first prompted them to cultivate the ground, to build houses, to found cities and commonwealths, and to invent and improve all the sciences and arts, which ennoble and embellish human life; which have entirely changed the whole face of the globe, have turned the rude forests of nature into agreeable and fertile plains, and made the trackless and barren ocean a new fund of subsistence, and the great high road of communication to the different nations of the earth.[16]

One oddity of this naturalistic account of human nature, to be discussed in a moment, is that some seem to have escaped subjection to nature's laws: wise philosophers can see through deceptions, even if they regard their workings as eminently beneficial. At this point, however, it is important to spell out the complete workings—social, psychological, and economic—of commercial society. Smith is very far from holding a simple and singular view of deception. He was well aware, to adopt modern terms, that goods themselves benefit their possessor most of all in terms of status.

[16] Ibid., book 4, chapter 1, 183–84.

From this derives Smith's image of the workings of commercial society. It is that of an endlessly moving escalator in which people chase those above them, so as to increase the respect of their fellows, only to find that those above them have moved on—or that there is another step on the escalator waiting to be mounted. A key assumption of this model is that of deference: it is part of human nature to seek to imitate those above one rather than to pull them back by socialist legislation of one sort or another. It is this that is the larger use of deception. Constantly running after a disappearing target is scarcely a recipe for human happiness, but it is, in Smith's view, one that will ensure both economic growth and, most important, social cohesion. The prospect of death will be diminished by the distractions involved in seeking distinction. How very great is the gap between civility and romanticism! Social peace follows competitive emulation.

So there is no "Adam Smith problem." The assumptions of his social psychology underlie the more limited concern with self-interest in *The Wealth of Nations*. The reason why self-interest is so strong is that the acquisition of wealth is the only way in which one can impress one's fellows. Keeping up with the Joneses makes commercial society tick. This broad judgment should not, however, hide both differences of emphasis or even changes between the two treatises, and two of these can usefully be mentioned. First, the savage irony that Smith directs at the masters of mankind has its origin in a distinctive view of morality—again, a prescriptive view of morality held somewhat awkwardly given that *The Theory of Moral Sentiments* is supposed to be a naturalistic account, a social psychology rather than an ethics.[17] What is particularly striking is that Smith values benevolence and altruism, and in part approves of capitalism, since increasing wealth will allow one to exercise charity. In all this, he is a long way from Mandeville: the workings of commercial society might be blind rather than planned, but the purpose of the whole was to civilize human beings—and certainly not to encourage their vices. Second, *The Theory of Moral Sentiments* makes much, almost in consequence, of the virtue of prudence, which is set very clearly against vanity. At this point one can detect a certain change in Smith's view of the social classes of his own day. Prudence is seen in the earlier book as residing among merchants and traders, who are, accordingly, best seen as the means by which commercial society will be established and maintained. *The Wealth of Nations* has a very different view. So, finally, we must turn to Smith's view of the state and to his account of theory and practice to show how he felt that the beneficial workings of commercial society could be maintained.

Dugald Stewart reported that Smith believed that a combination of "peace, easy taxes and a tolerable administration of justice" would allow commercial society to flourish.[18] Does this mean that Smith should be seen simply as the prophet of laissez-faire, believing, as did later neoclassical

[17] Smith does allow for the possibility that sentiments can be corrected, but his main prescriptive point concerns the role of the statesman who "contents himself with moderating what he cannot annihilate without great violence" (*Theory of Moral Sentiments*, part 6, chapter 2, 232–33).

[18] D. Stewart, "Account of the Life and Writings of Adam Smith, LL.D.," in A. Smith, *Essays on Philosophical Subjects* ([1793] Oxford: Clarendon Press, 1980), 322.

economists and their opponent Karl Marx, that the state should wither away? Many recent accounts of Smith, particularly by radical neoliberals, have made this claim. There is something to the claim, but a proper appreciation shows that Smith's desire for a state restrained in some ways is counterbalanced by his desire for one that is rather active in other matters. That a "tolerable" administration of justice is no small thing can be demonstrated without more ado by considering the functions of the state.

Most obviously, Smith had absolutely no illusions that a commercial society could survive without defense, nor did he think that the spread of commerce would itself guarantee peace. Smith seems equally traditional, and properly the favorite of the radical Right, in specifying the key internal function of the state.

> Civil government, so far as it is instituted for the security of property, is in reality instituted for the defence of the rich against the poor, or of those who have some property against those who have none at all.[19]

Against this sentiment must be set both his sympathy for labor and his dislike of the rich. This can be seen particularly clearly in his insistence that the state should provide public works necessary for society as a whole and for commerce in particular. One interesting passage even suggests that higher taxes at turnpikes should be levied on the ostentatiously rich: Smith's admiration was limited to the sober and intel-

---

[19] Smith, *Wealth of Nations*, book 5, chapter 1, 715.

ligent members of the commercial aristocracy of his time, and his dislike of the vanity of mere wastrels was strong. More important, Smith envisaged a rather large role, in spite of some of his later defenders, for the state in the public provision of infrastructure and education. Crucially, basic education should be generally available, and indeed demanded: both economy and society would benefit from a trained and active people. Education enlarged horizons that might well be cramped by the division of labor. In a famous passage, Smith suggested that endless specialization might result in a sort of "mental mutilation" that would make men less vigorous because so thoroughly cramped. Education was one answer to that problem. But there was another answer, and it is one that brings him close to the tradition of civic virtue to which he was generally opposed.[20] The state should insist on service in a militia. Even if not militarily necessary, active service would encourage fitness and so ensure that mental horizons were not too limited. There is a final function of the state. In an extremely interesting discussion of religion, he took issue with Hume's theory, best expressed in his *The Natural History of Religion*, that the way to combat dangerous enthusiasm was to allow an established church to stay in place, from which position it would become more and more inoffensive as more and more corrupt. Smith disliked monopolies, including that of the Anglican establishment, and proposed instead controlling enthusiasm by means of plu-

[20] Hanley and Forman-Barzilai have emphasized Smith's move toward the tradition of civic virtue in his later years as he became increasingly anxious about social cohesion, with the sentiments involved being visible in the final additions to the 1790 edition of *The Theory of Moral Sentiments*.

ralism. He allowed—almost advocated—radical, enthusiastic, and intolerant sects, but merely wished that there be many of them: multiplication would lead to a balance of power, and balance to the removal of any threat to society. But not everything could be left to this mechanism. Most obvious, the state needed to provide frequent public entertainment:

> The state, by encouraging, that is by giving entire liberty to all those who for their own interest would attempt, without scandal or indecency, to amuse and divert the people by painting, poetry, musick, dancing; by all sorts of dramatic representations and exhibitions, would easily dissipate, in the greater part of them, that melancholy and gloomy humour which is almost always the nurse of popular superstition and enthusiasm. Publick diversions have always been the objects of dread and hatred, to all the fanatical promoters of those popular frenzies.[21]

And a final antidote to enthusiasm remains the traditional one: that of the study of science and philosophy.

These considerations return us to the occasions when we have found Smith allowing for the importance of wisdom and reason, even though commercial society is seen to work essentially as a mechanical system. This is not an occasional inconsistency. *The Wealth of Nations* is advertised as "a handbook for the legislator," and book 4 of that treatise

---

[21] Smith, *Wealth of Nations*, book 5, chapter 1, 796.

makes it particularly clear why this is necessary. Merchants
and traders were, as noted, no true friends to the market
principle: they sought to gain special privileges from the
state that would give them rents sufficient to avoid adjusting
to the laws of supply and demand. These demands found
their larger expression in the policy of mercantilism. This
seemed to ensure security but in fact did no such thing: its
restraints on trade diminished the general good. The public
suffered as the few benefited. These comments show once
again Smith's criticism of what the propertied might do.
Hence, an absolutely key presupposition of his whole system is that the state remains in the hands of the wise and
disinterested. If both rich and poor are to be served, the
state must never be the mere instrument of the bourgeoisie.
It must remain autonomous, free from special interests and
thereby capable of thinking in the long term rather than the
short. It is for these people that Smith wrote. This political
class was the mechanism by which Smith felt his vision
could be realized.

The power and sophistication of Smith's thought seem
ever more impressive. To this appreciation must be added
the continuing relevance of much of his analysis of capitalism. Smith was right to insist that the secret of capitalist society was productivity. Equally, his idea that cohesion within
capitalism is achieved by means of chasing the person higher
up on a never-ending escalator remains a meaningful image
to this day. "Keeping up with the Joneses" remains central to
modern society. Smith's general viewpoint has received
striking confirmation from modern sociology. Most of us do
not conduct our lives or lay political claims on the basis of

abstract justice; rather, we compare ourselves with, and seek to catch, those to whom we are closest.[22] Finally, there is everything to be said for his concern with wealth. This is not merely a matter of providing decent sufficiencies. Recent research has shown that periods of economic growth do not just conceal the cracks of social conflict but rather bring in their train increased tolerance of all sorts.[23] So capitalism can have varied beneficial effects. But one must issue a warning at this point: the character of this social order can vary between generosity and meanness. It is also well to remember that Smith envisaged a version in which those at the bottom would have both negative resisting power and considerable skill—a world, in other words, based on a good deal of social inclusion.

[22] W. G. Runciman, *Relative Deprivation and Social Justice: A Study of Attitudes to Social Inequality in Twentieth-Century Britain* (London: Routledge and Kegan Paul, 1966).
[23] B. Friedman, *The Moral Consequences of Economic Growth* (New York: Alfred A. Knopf, 2005).

CHAPTER 3

How Best to Rule

Although Machiavelli is very often seen as a bad man, he is without a peer when it comes to teaching us how best to rule, a formulation designed to be ambiguous. I will bracket (at least for now) recent scholarship on the Florentine's republicanism—that is, the Machiavelli of *The Discourses*, the prophet of active citizenship and liberty—so as to concentrate on the adviser to princes. *The Prince* is concerned most of all with how to hold new territory, from which derive various principles of rule that led to Machiavelli gaining his reputation for evil. I have always had a divided view about this. On the one hand, there is a very great deal to be said for the view that politics is not moral, that its language is violence, and that it is a mistake to enter this world with a view to saving one's soul. In this matter Machiavelli's great descendants are Max Weber and Raymond Aron, both of whom wrote on the nature of the political with enormous force.[1] On the other hand, and perhaps because of this very understanding, it seems to me that there *is* much to approve morally in some of the points made by this purportedly bad

[1] M. Weber, "Politics as a Vocation," in *From Max Weber,* ed. H. H. Gerth and C. W. Mills ([1919] New York: Oxford University Press, 1948); R. Aron, *Mémoires* (Paris: Julliard, 1983), 22–23.

man. Machiavelli is right to insist that it is dangerous to seek to please too easily, to dispense goodies of one sort or another to the extent of bankrupting the state, thereby leading to arbitrary policies later on that are likely to create resentment and opposition. The more general point that Machiavelli makes in connection with this is that—to use modern words—politics do not matter most of the time for most citizens. Hence, any injury, any act of visceral coercion, should be inflicted at the start of a period of rule, so that it can then be forgotten during the extended periods of benign and regular stability that can follow.

This is the insight that leads to the call for civility in political life. The principle is best stated bluntly: political integration is the best route to order because softer political rule de-radicalizes. Civility is desirable, to put the point with reference to another supposedly nasty theorist, for Hobbesian reasons. Let me try to prove this case with reference to the entry of the people onto the political stage, both as classes and nations.

The most obvious, appropriate, and helpful place to begin when considering class is with Karl Marx, the greatest theorist of socialism. His expectation, and that of most Marxists in the years before the First World War, was clear: workers had no countries and so would inevitably be forced to unite as a solidarity class because of the inherent contradictions of the capitalist mode of production. In retrospect, we can see that the decision of workers to fight for their countries in 1914 was the first piece of writing on the wall that indicated the limits to the secular religion that is Marxism. But what matters here is something entirely different—namely, the variation in working-class behavior in the years before the onset of war.

Let us construct an imaginary scale of radicalism or political consciousness—as we must if we wish to be true to historical experience—and then turn to an explanation of its character.[2] At one end of such a scale is the United States, bereft of any mass socialist movement then and now. More radicalism is apparent in British politics with the emergence of the Labour Party in the early years of the twentieth century. But the radicalism of British workers was not deep, as can be seen by looking at two cases at the other end of the scale. Marx's greatest hopes were reserved for German workers, which is not surprising, as they possessed genuine political consciousness, expressed in 1912 in the electoral surge of the Socialist Party. Samuel Gompers and Arthur Henderson knew of Marxist ideas but resisted them as foreign and dangerous; in contrast, Marx's ideas were well known to many manual workers in Germany. Still, the farthest point on the scale belongs to Russian rather than to German workers. The point can be made straightforwardly: the workers of Saint Petersburg and Moscow put up barricades in the streets in 1917, which created the situation of dual power, famously described by Trotsky in his *History of the Russian Revolution*. These workers were genuinely revolutionary, prepared to act without intellectual guidance, and clearly less respectable and orderly than their German colleagues. These staccato points lead to a single conclusion: Marx was wrong, even for

[2] This scale is based on M. Mann, *The Sources of Social Power*, vol. 2, *The Rise of Classes and Nation-States, 1760–1914* (Cambridge: Cambridge University Press, 1993), chapters 15, 17, and 18.

his own time. There was no single working class, but rather working classes of particular countries. Let us see by country what was involved so that the variation can then be properly explained.

Workers in the United States were militant at the industrial level but lacked any alternative political consciousness because the state was, so to speak, their own: virtually all white males in the United States gained the vote in the 1830s, the age of Andrew Jackson. Doubtless there were other factors: class solidarity was undermined by immigrant labor, while one should not discount Werner Sombart's insistence that socialism in America drowned on the reefs of roast beef and apple pie.[3] Still, the other cases suggest that the nature of the political regime is the key variable. Thus, in Britain the moderation encouraged by the granting of trade union rights, but not votes for all manual workers, was interrupted by the 1902 Taff Vale court decision, which seemed to threaten them. The Labour Party resulted from this moment of putative repression. But any further move toward greater radicalism was prevented by the softer regime of the Liberal governments in the decade before the war, not least in its restoration of union rights. Equally, regime behavior best explains the radical cases. Antisocialist laws in Germany from 1878–90 meant that workers were forced to take on the state precisely because their industrial rights were curtailed. But imperial Germany was a *Rechtsstaat*, and this encouraged

---

[3] I. Katznelson and A. Zolberg, eds., *Working-Class Formation: Nineteenth-Century Patterns in Western Europe and the United States* (Princeton: Princeton University Press, 1988); W. Sombart, *Why Is There No Socialism in the United States?* ([1906] London: Macmillan, 1976).

legalistic, respectable politics. Imperial Russia was, of course, very different, autocratic and arbitrary rather than merely authoritarian. The fact that one might be shot for distributing leaflets encouraging a strike meant that the regime had to be destroyed. A necessary caution must be entered here, not least as it so massively supports the general argument. Adapting a phrase of Sartre helps capture the point. Russian workers had existences rather than any single essence. When the regime seemed open to the granting of rights, as in the early part of the century, radicalism declined markedly.[4] Lenin in effect wrote about those moments in *What Is to Be Done?*, his classic 1903 analysis of workers who were lacking political consciousness and so stuck in economism that a vanguard party was necessary if revolution was to be achieved. It was the abrupt ending of such political openings that drove workers to revolution without, as Lenin had suggested, the intervention of a vanguard party of intellectuals.

What is going on is clear. Workers jumped at the chance of reform rather than revolution, preferring to gain industrial benefits through union activity rather than risk being shot at on the barricades. So the character of working-class movements derived more from the nature of the political regime with which they interacted than from capitalist social relations. From this derives the point that matters: political inclusion contained—even tamed—working-class demands. It takes a very great deal to make working classes radical, let alone revolutionary—indeed, I can only really think of Russian workers before 1914, Protestant workers

[4] T. McDaniel, *Autocracy, Capitalism and Revolution in Russia* (Berkeley: University of California Press, 1988).

in Northern Ireland setting up barricades against power-sharing agreements in 1974, and the Polish workers of Solidarity as true political agents. Clearly, it is not capitalism that occasions violent conflict from below. Two qualifications need to be made concerning the highly simplified picture that has been presented. The first is historical. Elite treatment of working classes changed markedly after the First World War, with fascist regimes sometimes seeking to mobilize rather than to contain popular pressure. The second qualification concerns liberalism itself. It is important to remember that there were in fact two sides to liberal behavior. If one side allowed entry into politics, another side was capable of extreme viciousness toward small groups of extremists. The British state sent Chartist leaders to Australia, while worker deaths in the United States in the nineteenth century were second only to those in czarist Russia.[5] This complete strategy of liberalism in practice—at once offering an opening to the many while seeking to crush the few—is, of course, entirely in accord with the spirit of *The Prince*.

The same structure of argument applies to nations as to classes. In this intellectual field, we most certainly face an essentialist definition of nationalism, and one of great power and interest.[6] Ernest Gellner, the greatest theorist of nationalism, was wont to claim that one should assimilate or get one's own state, given that the only remaining alternative was to be killed. It is not hard to see that such a view derives from a thinker with a Jewish background (or, to be precise,

[5] Mann, *Sources*, chapters 15 and 18.
[6] E. A. Gellner, *Nations and Nationalism* (Oxford: Blackwell, 1983).

with a Jewish background imposed upon him) who had experienced the full horrors of the twentieth century's darkest continent.[7] Hence, his definition of nationalism stresses the need for each state to have a single culture, and each culture to have its own state. But this is not correct, at least in the terms that Gellner had set for himself, that is, as a general theory of nationalism. A superior alternative view stresses the very varied arrangements that have allowed different ethnicities and nations to live together in peace. The key principle here is very clear, and it is best expressed in terms of Albert Hirschman's *Exit, Voice and Loyalty*.[8] When a nation is denied voice—that is, when it is faced by a state that denies it cultural rights and political representation—secessionist exit becomes attractive, even necessary. Allowing voice, in contrast, can produce loyalty, thereby undermining secessionist drives. This is to say that different nations can live under a single political roof, as long as institutions and rights are established that allow the nations to prosper and survive. The key point that deserves emphasis here concerns the drivers of nationalism. Gellner had secession in mind in his famous parable of Ruritanians seeking to escape from Megalomania. But it was the behavior of Megalomania when trying to build a nation-state out of disparate elements—that is, of the elite, often radical in character—that helped to create demands for secession. Once again the character of movements resulted from the nature of the state with which they interacted. Some illustrations help make this clear.

---

[7] J. A. Hall, *Ernest Gellner: An Intellectual Biography* (London: Verso, 2010).
[8] A. O. Hirschman, *Exit, Voice and Loyalty: Response to Decline in Firms, Organizations and States* (Cambridge, MA: Harvard University Press, 1970).

One can begin with the classic case of the Czechs in the nineteenth century.[9] There was nothing inevitable about the creation of a Czech nation-state. Very much to the contrary, virtually every Czech national leader in the nineteenth century merely sought for cultural autonomy under the protection of the Hapsburgs. The logic to this position was very clearly articulated by František Palacký in 1848 when arguing for a Slav Congress in Prague—in opposition, of course, to the liberal meeting held in Frankfurt at that time. The Czechs feared being absorbed by Germany and were quite as afraid of Russia. If Austria did not exist, Palacký argued, it would have been necessary to invent her. The Czech national movement was not particularly radical; that is, it did not seek independence, so long as there was sufficient hope that the Hapsburgs would allow for cultural autonomy within their empire. For long periods there was every reason to believe that such hopes were realistic: linguistic and educational rights were granted, as was a measure of self-government. In the last analysis, however, the Hapsburgs balked at the granting of real autonomy: in the early years of the First World War it became clear that the constitutional monarchy for which the Czechs longed was to be denied. It was these circumstances that finally convinced Tomáš Masaryk that national independence had to be sought.

Even cursory reference to other cases makes it clear that there is nothing peculiar about the Czechs. I have been witness to exactly the same considerations in Quebec. The core liberalism of the Canadian state makes it very hard indeed to mobilize sufficient support for genuine independence, es-

[9] P. Bugge, *Czech Nation-Building, National Self-Perception and Politics, 1780–1914* (Aarhus: University of Aarhus, 1994).

pecially now that the French language is securely protected in Quebec. This is not to say that secession is impossible. What would be needed to create secession—and what independentist leaders continually seek—is some insult, some moment of repression that will make those who wobble believe that voice is denied to such an extent that exit has become absolutely necessary. The gut instinct, so far at least, of the rest of Canada has been to offer accommodations and defuse the situation with endless fuzzy civility. The same cards seem to be present in the relations between Scotland and England. Scottish nationalism gained some force as the result of the long period of interventions, especially in local government, of a Conservative government for which Scots had not voted. Devolution defused the situation, albeit Tony Blair's idiotic comment that real powers were not involved undermined the sensible accommodations being institutionalized. So the Scots, like the Quebecois, now have rights and multiple identities, and only normally wish for more if they can maintain existing links. They wish, to make use of an old Quebecois joke, for total independence within a united country. This can change, but only if pressure from the majority forces the minority into a corner from which it feels it must escape.

The general view being put forward is sufficiently novel as to deserve restatement by recalling the sociological insights of Ralf Dahrendorf's *Class and Class Conflict in Industrial Societies*. Dahrendorf's opposition to the Parsonian view of societies as held together by normative consensus led him to produce a series of abstract propositions about the nature of social conflict. The particular claim of interest here concerns the intensification of conflict. A single conflict is, so to speak, trivial and manageable. Real intensity results when different types of conflict are layered on top of one another.[10] An example given by Dahrendorf himself remains useful. French society has seen intense political conflict because religious and political divisions were layered on top of each other. To be on the left meant that one would inevitably be anticlerical, for those on the right received the backing of the Catholic Church. The underlying point remains that conflict diffuses through society unless state actions concentrate matters. Differently put, political civility can defuse tensions throughout society, thereby creating fundamental political stability.

Dahrendorf's principle can easily be illustrated with reference to the field with which he was purportedly concerned; namely, that of modern class conflict. Consider Solidarity. The fact that Polish workers were not allowed to have their own unions meant that they had to "take on" the state, because politics and economics were combined in actually existing socialism. The extraordinary consequence of this was that a group of workers in a nearly defunct industry did a very great deal to destroy the socialist state of Poland—thereby putting one of the nails in the Soviet model, and perhaps in socialism more generally. The point being made—that conflict diffuses through society unless it is artificially concentrated—can be reinforced by considering class conflict in modern Britain. I remember claiming in the early Thatcher years that any massive increase in un-

[10] R. Dahrendorf, *Class and Class Conflict in Industrial Societies* (Stanford, CA: Stanford University Press, 1959), chapter 6.

employment caused by her policies would surely lead to protest on a very large scale. Unemployment surged, but without much popular reaction. The answer to this conundrum lay most immediately in the fact that the unemployed lost union support, and tended moreover to be older—together with the state's intelligent provision of various social programs for the young. But something much larger was at issue. Social contracts between labor, capital, and the state have as a side effect the politicizing of industrial relations— they make the state responsible for levels of employment and give workers the right of access to political power. Margaret Thatcher abolished this connection, the world of "beer and sandwiches" in Downing Street: levels of employment resulted from the impersonal forces of global capitalism, held to be beyond the power of any state to control.[11]

That the principle in question has reached beyond the sociology of classes and nations can be shown by a cursory look at important recent work on the sociology of revolutions. The flavor of such work is neatly captured in the title of a leading treatise in the field, Jeff Goodwin's *No Other Way Out*.[12] Being shot at, tortured, and imprisoned is so terrifying that people seek to avoid it at all costs. But when it is not possible to escape such treatment, and when life can be dangerous in any case, people do become revolutionaries. The absence of the ability to participate in poli-

---

[11] K. Bradley and A. Gelb, "The Radical Potential of Cash Nexus Breaks," *British Journal of Sociology* 31 (1980).

[12] J. Goodwin, *No Other Way Out: States and Revolutionary Movements, 1945–91* (Cambridge: Cambridge University Press, 2001).

tics turns people into revolutionaries: normal politics is consequently a safety valve, diminishing the intensity of conflict. A member of the traditional elite of his society, Václav Havel only moved into outright opposition because there was no other way to be heard. The analytic point is clear: mere social relations do not explain the incidence of revolution. Thus, capitalist social relations and/or levels of poverty in Central America cannot explain the incidence of revolution for the simple reason that these conditions were essentially similar throughout the region, with revolution occurring in some rather than in other countries, for example, in Nicaragua rather than in Costa Rica. One factor that explains this should now be obvious to us: Costa Rica has a long history of liberal politics, in contrast to the Nicaragua of Somoza—which excluded and so radicalized another member of another elite family, Daniel Ortega. If here, too, the basic principle of civility in politics gains support, it is important to note that Goodwin's complete account pays attention to one further factor. Liberalism most certainly did not characterize Salvador, but that country avoided revolution. What distinguished Salvador from Nicaragua was the presence of genuinely meritocratic, and truly vicious, forces of coercion, in contrast to the nepotistic, "Sultanist" arrangements within Nicaragua. Pure force can sustain a regime, leading in the Salvadorean case to a period of brutal civil war. Nonetheless, the Weberian point—that force is less stable in the long run than legitimate power—remains true, with contemporary Salvador gaining real stability only in the last years when liberal openings have been created.

Let us turn away from these considerations and back to the historical record. It takes but a moment to realize how terribly Europe managed the entry of the people onto the political stage. Workers were radicalized in both imperial Germany and imperial Russia, which caused political difficulties in the former and a revolution in the latter that led to horrors that have still not been fully recorded. Nationalism was equally radicalized by state behavior. If nationalism was not the sole cause of war in 1914, it certainly added to the range and intensity of conflict within Europe during its darkest days, between 1914 and 1945. The principle of one culture per state was fulfilled only by means of population transfer, ethnic cleansing, and mass murder, all habitually carried out in the midst of the fog of war. There is thus something altogether odd about Europe seeing itself as a fount of wisdom, prepared to offer advice to the developing world. All in all, the elites of Europe exemplified human folly at its worst.

Nonetheless, Europe has now firmly established liberal democratic rule, and it is important to locate some elements of that achievement before turning to one surprising but very substantial achievement of some parts of the developing world. A foundation of the stability established by postwar European liberal democracy has been the role played by the United States. European history has been witness to endless wars of an increasingly destructive character in the industrial age. The United States solved Europe's security problem—and solves it still.[13] Beyond this, however, are factors internal

[13] J. A. Hall, "Europe: Banalities of Success," in *International Relations Theory and Regional Transformation*, ed. T. V. Paul (Cambridge: Cambridge University Press, 2012).

to Europe itself. Two world wars provided the incentive, particularly on the part of the Franco-German condominium, to create that greater level of international cooperation within Europe that is the European Union. Here we have a second historic moment akin to the accords that ended the Thirty Years' War, when the experience of horror combined with stalemate led to the (re-)creation of civility. France had suffered three invasions from Germany in a single lifetime, and so changed its tactics—it could not win, so it embraced instead. And this symbolized the calculations of most European states, realizing that doing less, ceasing to seek to be complete power containers, created more.[14] Further, civil politics emerged from the discrediting of the extreme Left and the extreme Right, that is, of those forces that sought to make virtue the business of the state. The defeat of fascism was so total as to discredit it completely, with Christian democracy perhaps doing more than any other force to cement liberalism in postwar Europe. The extreme Left was not defeated in battle in the same manner; rather, the undermining of communist parties in Europe in the immediate postwar years had a good deal to do with American interventionist policies, but it was largely discredited by the events of 1956, and wholly so by the suppression of the Prague Spring. In these circumstances class compromise was possible, blessed above all by the golden years of economic growth characteristic of the belle epoque of postwar Europe.[15]

[14] A. Milward, *The European Rescue of the Nation-State* (Berkeley: University of California Press, 1992).
[15] A. Milward, *The Reconstruction of Western Europe, 1945–51* (Berkeley: University of California Press, 1984).

Europeans have a right to be proud of these postwar
achievements. But pride most certainly should not be excessive, as we can see if we turn from class to nation. There are
achievements in this area as well. Geopolitical order has allowed states to be less unitary, with real autonomy being
granted to regions of Britain and Spain. But the fundamental reason for the diminution of conflict over the national
question is altogether brutal. The national question no longer exists in most of Europe: it was "solved" by the horrors
of twentieth-century politics. Before 1914 perhaps sixty million Europeans lived in states ruled by people not cocultural
with themselves. This was reduced to perhaps twenty million by the creation of new states in 1918 and 1919.[16] Still,
many of those states had significant minorities within
them, and it took the Second World War to establish near-
complete national homogeneity in Central and Eastern Europe. We have, of course, witnessed the continuation of this
dreadful history in the third set of Balkan wars that followed the dissolution of Yugoslavia.

It is at this point that one can point to a marvelous development present in some parts of the developing world.
The almost total inability of Europeans to create political
regimes within which different nations can live and prosper stands in marked contrast to the situation elsewhere.
The classic and most important example is that of India,
whose situation is best understood with reference to the
political scientist David Laitin's superlative work on lin-

[16] M. Mann, "The Dark Side of Democracy: The Modern Tradition of Ethnic
and Political Cleansing," *New Left Review*, no. 235 (1999): 33.

guistic repertoires.[17] Active Indian citizenship requires linguistic capacity in three plus or minus one languages. Two languages that are clearly necessary are those of Hindi and English, both of which have all-India official status. But most people live within states that have their own language—for example, Tamil for Tamil Nadu. One needs capacity in only two languages when one's state is Hindi-speaking, but four languages if one happens to be a minority in a non-Hindi-speaking state, such as Tamil Nadu. Language is, of course, but one factor; still, it is a vital symbol, making India's success very remarkable indeed.[18] Some details and qualifications need to be added to this picture.[19] Support is given to the picture painted of India by the rather different behavior of that state in Kashmir: authoritarian rule there exacerbates secessionist feelings. In contrast, Tamil nationalism lost its secessionist drive because of the granting of rights.[20] Still, it is thanks to the observation of the principle of civility that this great part of the developing world has *not* followed the pattern of Europe's past. Accordingly, tens of millions of people have avoided violent deaths. The pacifying effects of civility

[17] D. Laitin, *Language Repertoires and State Construction in Africa* (Cambridge: Cambridge University Press, 1993).

[18] No claim is being made that the liberalism of language policy is the only factor responsible for political stability in India. The presence of an army that remains the backbone of the state, as well as a measure of unity bred by participation in a mass nationalist movement, clearly have enormous significance as well.

[19] A. Stepan, J. Linz, and Y. Yadav, *Crafting State-Nations: India and Other Multinational Democracies* (Baltimore: Johns Hopkins University Press, 2011).

[20] N. Subramanian, *Ethnicity and Popular Mobilization: Party Politics and Democracy in South India* (Oxford: Oxford University Press, 1999).

on the part of the state are confirmed once again, but a crucial misunderstanding must be avoided. Though there are a
significant number of countries in the developing world
that operate with linguistic regimes not dissimilar to those
of India, there is no denying the fact that many other states
have sought to copy the European route of national homogenization, often with disastrous consequences. But
India shows that a better way to rule is a possibility.

These comments about language suggest a final look at the
European situation. The European Union more or less possesses a linguistic regime similar to that of India, a two plus
or minus one repertoire—the language of one's state plus
English comprising the standard two, minus that if one is
English, with a third language necessary if one is a minority
within all national states except for Great Britain.[21] For that
reason, there is a sense in which Europe has now become an
Austria-Hungary that works—in part, though, because it has
few geopolitical ambitions that would require unitary state-
hood. But it takes just a moment to realize that problems
remain within Europe. Languages can be learned, allowing
several nations to live under the same political roof, but class
factors can play a role within nationalism. Specifically, it is
not easy to be truly fluent in another language, with capacities in writing as well as speaking. Class advantage, the ability
to take holidays in other countries and to send one's children
to summer schools in such countries, helps create linguistic
repertoires. One form of nationalism that seems to have
gained prominence in the early years of the new millennium

[21] D. Laitin, "The Cultural Identities of a European State," *Politics and Society* 25
(1997).

is that of the excluded, that is, those whose class background makes them wish to preserve the benefits of traditional nation-states. Tensions are developing between internationalism and domestic social cohesion. Civility in political life faces considerable new challenges that will require rethinking of some of its core components.[22] In conclusion, let me return to theoretical matters. The main claim has been that civil society "normally" operates according to its own logic, the insistence that political consciousness is created by the demands of an interfering state, and the discovery that inclusion can defang or contain radicalism. One thinker who stands close to the general argument is Max Weber. He was well aware that German workers had been turned in a radical direction by the regime's antisocialist laws, and his views on a reconstructed Germany made it quite clear that he thought a measure of inclusion would make them loyal to the regime.[23] It might seem that this makes him an exemplar of the position advocated here, but this is not quite so, for Weber despised political passivity. If workers had been unnecessarily radicalized, his fundamental belief was that loyalty to Germany should be active rather than passive—through endorsement of the national principle that he himself held so dear. More generally, his view of democracy emphasized the importance of charismatic leadership, the highlighting of which would allow

[22] J. A. Hall, "Nationalism Might Change Its Character, Again," in *Nationalism and Globalisation: Conflicting or Contemporary?*, ed. D. Halikiopoulou and S. Vasilopoulou (London: Routledge, 2012).

[23] M. Weber, "Parliament and Government in a Reconstructed Germany," in his *Economy and Society*, ed. and trans. G. Roth and C. Wittich ([1922] Berkeley: University of California Press, 1978).

movement rather than stagnation in a society. There is also
some resonance of the argument with the views of Tocqueville. As we will see in chapter 9, the great French liberal certainly stressed in multiple ways that social forces gain their
character from the nature of the states within which they
are embedded. A rather neglected example of this concerns
civil associations. These were dangerous in France, as they
were conspiratorial and convinced of their right to rule,
whereas in the United States they served as the training
ground for responsible citizenship. The difference was easily
explained. When associations were forced underground,
they became radicalized and prone to believe that they represented the popular will; such delusions were removed
by openness, which transmitted a sense of reality.[24] But
Tocqueville has severe and understandable misgivings about
the position advocated, as we can see by turning to its great
weakness.

The case that has been made is not altogether nice, being,
so to speak, left-handed or paradoxical in endorsing practices almost in opposition to the spirit in which they were
created and for which they were intended. Perhaps this does
not matter. Surely it is better to be intellectually powerful
than politically correct, especially in an intellectual environment in which hope so often triumphs over historical experience. But it is also good to note the fundamental presupposition that civil society can and will operate on its own, if
the state allows that to happen. This is accurate sociology in
normal times. But times are not always normal. The classic

---

[24] A. de Tocqueville, *Democracy in America*, trans. H. Mansfield and D. Winthrop ([1835 and 1840] Chicago: University of Chicago Press, 2000), 170–71.

instance of this not being so is, of course, that of Weimar Germany. Political order could not be achieved passively, by allowing economic growth to paper over political cracks. In these circumstances, the lack of positive enthusiasm came to matter. So in the end we are returned to the Machiavelli of the *Discourses*, and to Tocqueville's great warning about self-interest properly understood.[25] Negative rule is not always enough.

This is a good moment to consider the criticism of the general argument made by Ralph Schroeder in his important *An Age of Limits: Social Theory for the 21st Century*.[26] He draws a contrast between the radicalism present in the work of Michael Mann and the liberalism argued for here, and suggests that the former has a structural base in working-class movements that the latter altogether lacks. There is both exaggeration and truth here. There is probably less difference between these two positions than is suggested. The working class is no longer much of a structural base, while I am totally happy, as the comment made about negative rule indicates, to acknowledge the contributions made by those who struggled for citizenship. What matters for both parties he identifies is the importance of political struggle within bounds; neither romanticizes revolution. Further, it will become clear that I am certainly at one with Mann in a different matter, believing that much social change results from geopolitical outcomes rather than from domestic social life. But Schroeder is correct when insisting that civility

[25] Ibid., 514–17.
[26] R. Schroeder, *An Age of Limits: Social Theory for the 21st Century* (Basingstoke: Palgrave Macmillan, 2013).

has no secure structural base. That is a core presumption of this book: when we have it, we should cherish it. This is not to say that this book is bereft of advocacy or totally without any thought as to forces that strengthen and extend civility. On the contrary, civil behavior by elites has crucial societal consequences, and it can be recommended on the grounds of self-interest. And one can go a little further. Adam Smith's emphasis on the crucial importance of human capital seems even more relevant as production structures change, with knowledge becoming more relevant as well. Necessity is never necessarily the mother of invention; rather, changes have to be recognized for responses to be made. But at times one can see elite intelligence in action, based on the recognition of necessity: Danish elites, for example, seem determined to include the people within society, to make social democracy increasingly more effective, so that their small nation can survive.[27] Larger states are less vulnerable, and they possess more power, so desirable changes in political economy are by no means uniform. And against optimism must be set those occasions when one sees political elites acting with absolute folly, as in 1914 and perhaps now in Europe when imposing austerity in a way that will, for sure, prove to be self-defeating. This last thought simply underlines the fact that civility is not guaranteed.

[27] J. L. Campbell and J. A. Hall, "Defending the Gellnerian Premise: Denmark in Historical and Comparative Perspective," *Nations and Nationalism* 16 (2010).

CHAPTER 4

Entry and Exit

Praise of civility can be dreadfully "wet," as noted, offering little more than the injunction to be nice. That has not been the case so far in this book: the origins of civility lay in viciousness, while its maintenance largely rests on competitive emulation and depoliticization. Beyond all this, however, stands the serious but less obvious weakness identified by John Murray Cuddihy in *The Ordeal of Civility*.[1] This brilliant book casts a searching light on "civility" by analyzing how outsiders experienced its standards, with concentration in his case on the Jewish experience in the modern era.

Let me proceed inductively, by means of an example that will lead to more general reflections.[2] One of the greatest intellects of the postwar era, Ernest Gellner was born in 1925 and raised in Prague to a family with a Jewish background (felt more by the mother than the father) and within a world in which the greatest loyalty was owed to the Czechoslovak state headed by Tomáš Masaryk, to whom particular allegiance was given because he had fought against

[1] J. M. Cuddihy, *The Ordeal of Civility: Freud, Marx, Levi-Strauss and the Jewish Struggle with Modernity* (Boston: Beacon Press, 1974).
[2] J. A. Hall, *Ernest Gellner: An Intellectual Biography* (London: Verso, 2010), especially chapter 3.

anti-Semitism. Gellner's identity was more Czech than Jewish, but the latter identity was present—first in his schooling
and massively so when it was imposed upon him by the horrors of mid-twentieth-century Europe, which drove him into
exile in 1939. After fighting in the war, and going into what
seemed like permanent exile in Britain in 1946, this brilliant
and highly ambitious young man wanted to "get in," to succeed. But getting in was not so easy. The English upper classes
of the time painted him as Eastern European, too clever by
half and far too interested in sex—or so he felt that he was
seen, and actually portrayed in an unpublished novel by one
of his close friends. If there was wry amusement for Gellner
in this, followed by an embrace of homelessness, there was
also at times very great resentment. Some of the latter sentiment was directed at his colleague, Michael Oakeshott, who
disliked "rationalists" and waxed lyrical about the benefits of
tradition. Tradition would, of course, permanently exclude
those who did not know the rules, so Gellner loved to mock-
ingly quote passages from Oakeshott, such as this, which so
clearly exemplified a civility that was narrow at best and rac-
ist at worst:

> Like a foreigner or a man out of his social class, he is
> bewildered by a tradition and a habit of behavior of
> which he knows only the surface; a butler or an obser-
> vant house-maid has the advantage of him.[3]

[3] M. Oakeshott, *Rationalism in Politics and Other Essays* (London: Methuen,
1962), 31, cited in E. A. Gellner, *Legitimation of Belief* (Cambridge: Cambridge
University Press, 1974), 4.

Further resentment was shown toward Isaiah Berlin, whose background was not dissimilar to his own, on the grounds that he had accepted such local standards, thereby abandoning his allegiance to truth and reason.

In the course of the nineteenth century, the closed world of the ghettos was coming to an end. Interest could be shown to this world, not least by Franz Kafka, but in the end there was a general movement away from it. Many sought complete assimilation, hoping to merge into the local norms, often by changing name and religion. But insiders could often recognize those wanting to get in, and so could make life difficult for them: differently put, anti-Semitism increased in force throughout the century. And the problem was not faced just once; rather, the influx of the less-educated Jews from the East made the dilemma continual, often to the irritation of those who felt themselves to have already assimilated successfully. In these circumstances another general route emerged: the call for universal standards by thinkers with Jewish backgrounds. Cuddihy's claim is that Marx and Freud took this route. An equally stunning example is that of the large number of early Bolsheviks of Jewish background whose discovery that they were not wanted in nationalist movements led them to become left-wing empire-savers.[4] Then there is the famous treatise by Karl Popper, *The Open Society and Its Enemies*, a superlative call for universalism filled with

---

[4] L. Riga, "The Ethnic Roots of Class Universalism: Rethinking the 'Russian' Revolutionary Elite," *American Journal of Sociology* 114 (2008).

distaste for nationalism of any sort. This suggests a final
option, that of Jewish self-identification and pride, seen
above all in Zionism. One reason for this option is
straightforward: specifically, that universalism failed, and
many of those who called for it were killed.[5] Just as important is the feeling that denying one's roots was a form of
self-mutilation, with those so doing often being accused of
"self-hatred."[6] This last sentiment can amount to such communal disapproval as to make it hard for one to leave, an
additional burden to the obvious problem of communities
not wanting to allow entry.

Gellner's social theory as a whole endlessly revolves
around the tension caused by the importance of context-
free inquiry and the human desire for a measure of cultural
belonging, with his real claim to fame lying in his attack on
any thinker who embraced only one of these poles rather
than seeking some way to swim between them.[7] I certainly
share his general philosophical position, and insist on underlining the certain fact that the dilemma is real—and with
application well beyond that of the Jewish community. But
the purpose of introducing the issue here remains simple. Is
"civility" in fact so loaded with cultural flavor and baggage
that it is not neutral and desirable? This supposition would
certainly add real bite to the question. Might it not be the
case, as one reader of the manuscript of this book suggested,

[5] M. Hacohen, "Karl Popper in Exile: The Viennese Progressive Imagination
and the Making of *The Open Society*," *Philosophy of Social Sciences* 26 (1990).
[6] P. Birnbaum, *The Geography of Hope: Exile, the Enlightenment, Disassimilation*
(Stanford, CA: Stanford University Press, 2008).
[7] E. A. Gellner, *Language and Solitude: Wittgenstein, Malinowski and the Hapsburg Dilemma* (Cambridge: Cambridge University Press, 1998).

that my argument is terribly English? After the English civil war, something of a cultural norm arose in which it became impolite to talk about politics and religion, and possibly sex as well, which didn't leave much but the weather to animate conversation. And I can add the personal irritation of my partner, who at times insists, somewhat to my surprise, that life with an Englishman is by no means easy, for hints have to be taken as statements, while abhorrence is shown to open conflict.

The best way to gain some purchase on this issue is to analyze the general call for cultural pluralism (held to be desirable when contrasted to homogeneity), which is purportedly achievable only by force and held to be the result of the imposition of a particular, rather than a universal, set of standards. This seems to be the language of tolerance, even liberty. Let a thousand flowers bloom! Surely no decent person could argue to the contrary? I do claim decency, yet I reject a good deal of this general position. Mild jokes might be in order at the start. For one thing, it is noticeable that the cry for difference is uniform, singular, and homogeneous! For another, claims for difference often accompany assertions that the world is becoming globalized! More seriously, there is certainly a good deal to be said against difference insofar as it fades into complete relativism, surely the last refuge of the scoundrels of the modern world. The argument that follows can best be seen as offering generalized, sociological skepticism toward the claim that social processes are such that multicultural loyalties are replacing more national identities. But the center of attention focuses on an empirical comparison between the contemporary

United States and Europe, and leads to considerable praise for the American way of life.[8] Here is a situation in which, as we shall see, less is more.

Conceptual clarity can be gained by dissecting the celebrated notions of civic and ethnic nationalism, not least as this will suggest a schema that differentiates options of belonging. We should not accept everything that is implied in the formula ethnic/bad, civic/good. For one thing, there is nothing necessarily terrible about loyalty to one's ethnic group—and this sentiment in fact underlies the supposedly civic nationalism of the French. For another, civic nationalism is not necessarily nice: its injunction can be "join us or else." This was certainly true of the way in which Paris treated La Vendée during the early years of the Revolution, and it remains at the back of the contemporary "affaire des foulards." Put another way, civic nationalism may be resolutely hostile to diversity. This suggests the following scheme.[9]

---

[8] The emphasis on "contemporary" is deliberate and important. Slavery has been the great horror of the history of the United States, and its legacy remains powerful, as will be carefully stressed in the rest of this chapter. So the scope of generalizations made here is limited; it does not include a discussion of race.

[9] I recognize that this is a limited scheme, designed in largest part to contrast the situations of the United States and the European Union. Perhaps the biggest omission in the scheme is its failure to capture new transnational identities—that is, it does not reflect the new experience of migrants able to return to and communicate with their homeland with relative ease. The most interesting research on such immigrants suggests that they belong neither to their homeland nor to their new host country but rather sit interestingly, if uneasily, between both—a situation that happens to be my own. On this see *Towards a Transnational Perspective on Migration*, ed. N. Glick Schiller, L. Basch, and C. S. Blank (New York: New York Academy of Sciences, 1992); *The Changing Face of Home*, ed. P. Levitt and M. Waters (New York: Russell Sage Foundation, 2002); and S.

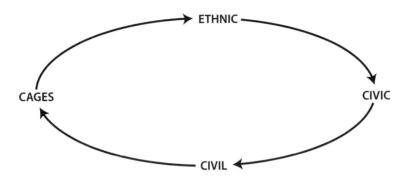

Moving clockwise around this circle allows a series of theoretical points to be made.

Ethnic nationalism is indeed repulsive when it is underwritten by relativist philosophies insisting that one should literally think with one's blood. Much less horrible is the combination of ethnic and civic nationalisms represented by France—that is, a world in which one is taken in or allowed in as long as one absorbs the culture of the dominant ethnic group. Civic nationalism becomes more liberal when it moves toward the pole of civility, best defined in terms of the acceptance of diverse positions or cultures.

Whether this last move is, so to speak, sociologically real can be measured by asking two questions. First, is the identity to which one is asked to accede relatively thin; that is, does it have at its core political loyalty rather than a collective memory of an ethnic group? It is helpful to remember in this context that the most interesting of Ernest Renan's views about the nature of nationalism was his claim that the success of any nation depended on its capacity to forget a

Vertovec, "Migrant Transnationalism and Modes of Transformation," *International Migration Review* 38 (2004).

good deal of the past.[10] Second, are rates of intermarriage high? In other words, is the claim that one can belong regardless of one's background borne out by the facts?

All this is obvious. Less so, perhaps, is a tension that lies at the heart of multiculturalism. In the interests of clarity, matters can be put bluntly. Multiculturalism properly understood *is* civil nationalism, the recognition of diversity. But that diversity is—needs to be, should be—limited by a consensus on shared values. Difference is acceptable only as long as group identities are voluntary, that is, insofar as identities can be changed according to individual desire. What is at issue is neatly encapsulated, as already noted, in the notion of caging. If multiculturalism means that groups have rights over individuals—if, for example, the leaders of a group have the power to decide to whom young girls of the community should be married—then it becomes repulsive. Such multiculturalism might seem liberal in tolerating difference, but it is in fact the illiberalism of misguided liberalism and diminishes life chances by allowing social caging. This view is, of course, relativist, and it is related to ethnic nationalism in presuming that one must think with one's group. Importantly, the link to ethnic nationalism may be very close indeed. If there are no universal standards, and ethnic groups are held to be in permanent competition, then it is possible, perhaps likely, that one group will seek to dominate another.

If these are ideal typical positions, a powerful stream of modern social theory in effect suggests that some have

[10] E. Renan, "What Is a Nation?," in *Becoming National: A Reader*, ed. G. Eley and R. G. Suny ([1882] Oxford: Oxford University Press, 1996).

greater viability than others. A series of thinkers, interestingly all liberal, have insisted that homogeneity, whether ethnic or civic, is a "must" if a society is to function effectively. John Stuart Mill made this claim when speaking about the workings of democracy, insisting that the nationalities question had to be solved in order for democracy to be viable.[11] The great contemporary theorist of democracy Robert Dahl has reiterated this idea.[12] The notion behind all this is straightforward. Human beings cannot take too much conflict, cannot put themselves on the line at all times and in every way. For disagreement to be productive in the way admired by liberalism, it must be contained—that is, it must take place within a frame of common belonging. To a great extent, the same insight underlies David Miller's view that national homogeneity is a precondition for generous welfare regimes.[13] This is correct: the generosity of Scandinavian countries rests on the willingness to give generously to people exactly like oneself. But the great theorist of the need for social homogeneity was, of course, Gellner, who argued that homogeneity was necessary so that industrial society can function properly. That Slovakia and the Czech Republic have prospered apart rather than suffering together might seem to support his view.

Skepticism has already been shown to the view that nations cannot live together under a single political roof. But a good deal more illumination on this issue, and on the pos-

[11] J. S. Mill, *Considerations on Representative Government* (London: Parker, Son and Bourn, 1861), chapter 16.
[12] R. Dahl, *Polyarchy* (New Haven: Yale University Press, 1977).
[13] D. Miller, *On Nationality* (Oxford: Clarendon Press, 1995).

sibility of civil nationalism, can be given by turning to the
United States and to Europe, a comparison in surprising
ways to the advantage of the former.

There are at least two obvious and powerful reasons for
turning to the United States. First, the United States deserves far more study than it receives, and not just in relation to the topic presently under analysis. For one thing,
America is the greatest power that the world has ever known.
At present it spends about 50 percent of the world total of
military expenditure, giving it continuing power over the
international market—that is, over such economic rivals as
Japan and the European Union. For another, it is the world
within which talk of difference is insistent, even deafening.
This may, of course, be no accident. The historic uniqueness
of the United States perhaps lies in the fact that it was
formed through immigration, that it is a polity created from
difference. Of course, that very formulation suggests that
America has been a melting pot, homogenizing the many
into a single unit. Was that true? Is it still true today?

The answer to that question must be wholly affirmative.[14]
But recognition of a sociological reality does not require
moral endorsement. Hence, consideration of the harsh side
of the melting pot is needed before turning to fundamen-
tally meritorious social practices that allow American nationalism to move beyond its dominant civic core toward
elements of genuine civility.

The United States is not a social world that favors diver-

[14] The arguments that follow are presented in greater detail in J. A. Hall and C.
Lindholm, *Is America Breaking Apart?* (Princeton: Princeton University Press,
1999).

sity. An initial consideration to that effect lies in the simple fact that white Anglo-Saxon settlers more or less exterminated the native population, thereby establishing their own hegemony.[15] African Americans received treatment nearly as vicious. Further, the creation of the new state placed a very strong emphasis on uniformity. For one thing, a Constitution was formed, a singular set of ideals created, which thereafter was held to be sacred.[16] For another, the United States was created by means of powerful acts, usually directed from below, of political cleansing. A significant section of the elite that had supported the Crown—in absolute numerical terms larger than those guillotined in France during the Revolution, and from a smaller population—was forced to leave.[17] Canada thereby gained an element of that anti-Americanism that comprises the key part of its national identity.

Perhaps the most striking general interpretation of American history and society—that proposed by scholars such as Richard Hofstadter, Daniel Bell, and Seymour Martin Lipset—is that which insists on the power of these initial ideas, of continuity through continuing consensus.[18] This is not quite right. If some alternatives were ruled out at the time of

[15] M. Mann, *The Dark Side of Democracy: Explaining Ethnic Cleansing* (Cambridge: Cambridge University Press, 2005).

[16] It may seem that the diversity allowed in religious practice contradicts the point being made. This is not really so, as is most evident once we note that Americans today trust those who have a religion—any religion—while showing suspicion toward those who have none.

[17] R. Palmer, *The Age of Democratic Revolution* (Princeton: Princeton University Press, 1959), 1:188–202.

[18] The clearest statement of this view is now S. M. Lipset, *American Exceptionalism* (New York: W. W. Norton, 1996).

foundation, others were eliminated as the result of historical events. The two most important examples deserve at least minimal attention.

First of all, we ought to remember that the United States remained unitary only as the result of a very brutal civil war. The Constitution had, of course, recognized the different interests of the slave-owning Southern states, but the difference between North and South grew in the early years of the Republic. The works of John Calhoun amount to a myth of hierarchy on the basis of which a new nation might have been formed. War destroyed that diversity, with Lincoln trying at the end of the conflict to create unity by means of such new institutions as Thanksgiving. Of course, the South did not lose its cultural autonomy simply as the result of defeat in war but maintained a key hold on federal politics well into the 1930s. Nonetheless, over time the South has lost its uniqueness, especially in recent years, as the result of political change and of population and industrial transfers from North to South. And in this general area of nationalism, it is well worth noting that there is no possibility of the United States becoming a multinational society. No one wants a second civil war of visceral intensity. Furthermore, Americans are overwhelmingly opposed to the idea that Spanish should be recognized as a second official language. The toughness of American civic nationalism was seen in the quip of Miriam A. Ferguson, the governor of Texas who opposed the introduction of bilingualism, that if "English was good enough for Jesus Christ, it ought to be good enough for the children of Texas." This is surely one element ensuring that Spanish is quickly being lost as a second language, as was the case for languages of other immigrant groups in the nineteenth century.

The second alternative vision was that of socialism, in one form or another. Revisionist history makes it equally clear that there was a genuine socialist stream of ideas and institutions in American history, represented most spectacularly in the militant unionism of the International Workers of the World. Further proof of the strength of working-class activism can be found in the bitterness of labor disputes, which resulted in a very large number of deaths, second only to those at the hands of the late czarist empire.

This is all to say that American ideals of individualism and enterprise were not so powerful or so widely shared as to rule out a challenge. Their ascendancy came about, as noted, for two fundamental reasons. On the one hand, the fact that citizenship had been granted early on meant that worker dissatisfaction tended to be limited, to be directed against industrialists rather than against the state, thereby limiting its overall power. On the other hand, and crucially for this argument, socialism was literally destroyed, as is made apparent by that very large number of working-class deaths. The recipe for social stability, as argued, is often the combination of political opening with absolute intolerance toward extremists. Certainly this mixture worked in the United States, ensuring that it would thereafter be bereft of any sort of social democratic tendency.

The rosier and milder face of the coin of American homogeneity can be seen at work in American ethnic relations. A warning should be issued before describing a remarkable American achievement. Everything that will be said excludes African Americans, whose position inside the United States remains heavily marked by racial discrimination. The hideousness of what is involved can be seen in situations where the vast majority of middle-class African Americans who strive to "get in" by being economically successful often experience bitterness when they discover that integration does not exist in the suburbs to which they move.[19] But for the majority of Americans, ethnic identity is now an option, not a destiny imposed from outside.[20] Rates of intermarriage are extremely high, not least for the first generation of Cuban Americans in Florida, more than 50 percent of whom marry outside their own group. Ethnic identity has little real content. It is permissible to graduate from kindergarten wearing a sari as long as one does not believe in caste—that is, as long as one is American. There are severe limits to difference.

Societies are complicated, so it makes sense to summarize what has been said by placing the United States at several points of the schema that has been provided. It is not the case that the United States has been completely free from ethnic nationalism. The colonists destroyed the native inhabitants. Furthermore, some part of the identity enshrined in the Constitution reflects the British background of the initial majority. Nonetheless, the United States does score firmly in the civic camp. The harshness of its civic culture can be seen in the destruction of alternative visions. But the United States has moved toward a civil position:

[19] Hall and Lindholm, *Is America Breaking Apart?*, chapter 10.
[20] M. Waters, *Ethnic Options: Choosing Ethnicities in America* (Berkeley: University of California Press, 1990).

American identity is less Anglo-Saxon than it was, given the capacity of Americans to create new national narratives with ease, while still more important are the astonishing high rates of intermarriage already described—for all but Afro-Americans, of course, whose life chances remain scandalously impoverished. In contrast to these points of reference, a particular absence must be very clearly set. All those books and treatises, the polemics of despair, asserting that the United States is falling apart because multiculturalism is becoming, in our terms, caging and illiberal are woefully misguided. It might very well be terrible were the relativism of politicized identity cages so complete as to destroy any sense of a common culture. But this is not the case. What matters about identity claims in the United States is that they are at once without content and so very generally made. They represent yet another moment of America's startling ability to create a common culture. This is a remarkable society, but it is not one of great difference and diversity. The powers of homogenization in the United States—deriving as much from Hollywood and consumerism, of course, as from the factors examined here—remain intact. The melting pot still works, but it has a particular character. Its homogeneity is "lite." There is little caging of ethnicity, and a rather small and happily ever-changing set of beliefs to which adherence is required. If one wished to criticize this achievement, it would be to stress how limited diversity is within the United States.[21] But one's worry in this regard

[21] M. Weinfeld (*Like Everyone Else . . . But Different: The Paradoxical Success of Canadian Jews* [Toronto: McClelland and Stewart, 2001], chapter 6) is aware of this, and makes much of the contribution of Jewish communities to genuine di-

fades when remembering that an exception to all this is, as
noted, race—an area in which there is a good deal of caging
and about which one further point must be made. Welfare
provision exists in the United States, but it is more limited
than in Europe *because* of race: the refusal to share with people judged not to be one's fellows, the result for many years
of the votes of the "Solid South," limited provisions and dis-
torted them in many ways.[22] To have this situation in such a
rich country is morally scandalous, but a sociologist must
also note that it makes it easy for immigrants to enter—they
have little to claim, and so cause limited resentment.

In contrast, there has been nothing "lite" about the European situation. Furthermore, critical problems exist today,
and this despite advances in some countries. Little will be
found here, as noted, to justify European anti-Americanism,
a continuing sentiment that is far too self-satisfied for its
own good.

It may be useful to preface the comments to be made by
highlighting, in different words, a point already made about
the nature of nationalism. Although it is well known that
the great theorists of nationalism came from the world of
Austria-Hungary, insufficient attention has been paid to
Sigmund Freud. What matters about his work is less the
particular views expressed in *Moses and Monotheism* than

---

versity because their traditions can at times be strong enough to maintain a
genuine way of life. He recognizes and endorses some limited amount of social
caging as necessary to community maintenance.
[22] I. Katznelson, *When Affirmative Action Was White: An Untold History of Racial Discrimination in Twentieth-Century America* (New York: W. W. Norton,
2005).

that an argument can be made on the basis of his view of the libido. That peculiar substance is seen to be sticky, capable of attaching itself to different objects, which then lend it a particular character. So it is with nationalism. This protean force is licentiously labile, gaining its character from the social forces with which it interacts. Let us consider three highly stylized, ideal typical moments of nationalism in modern European history, since to do so will advance the argument.

The first stage is that of simplicity and innocence. Nationalism was linked to liberalism. The Old Regime represented a common enemy. A typical figure in this regard is John Wilkes, the editor of the *North Briton* and the somewhat flawed champion of popular representation. To mention the Highland Clearances in Scotland is to note that nationalism at this time had some hideous moments of forced homogenization. Nonetheless, this period, best represented by Britain, was relatively benign. The sociology of the situation was simple: the state had come before the nation. The centralization of feudalism played a large part in the creation of a single language early on, to which varied groups acceded over a long period of time. The second stage is that of horror and viciousness. Here nation came before state in the composite monarchies of the Romanovs and the Hapsburgs. In these empires—and in that of the Ottomans—varied ethnic groups gained self-consciousness, thereby turning ethnic diversity into genuine multinationalism. This often made for great difficulties, notably when national and social inequalities were combined. Nonetheless, multinational arrangements were not necessarily doomed by socioeconomic pressures coming from below. On the contrary, many nations merely sought the affirmation of their historic liberties, with the Slavs being somewhat scared of secession given their geopolitical placement between Russia and Germany. But exit became attractive in the course of time because of state policies of linguistic and cultural homogenization that were designed to copy the leading powers by making nation-states out of diverse materials. The third period is the one of modesty described in chapter 3. This is the world of economic interdependence, of trade rather than of heroic adventure.[23] This is not for a moment to accept the claim, made so often these days, that the nation-state is dead.[24] Still, the mood of the nation-state has changed. Abandoning the attempt to be complete power containers has increased security. Doing less has proved to give more.

One should and can claim that a great contemporary European achievement, aided by the United States, is the newfound ability of several countries to live together without recourse to war. Competition between these states remains, of course, not least given the presence of different political economies within Europe and of different standards of success between them, but this does not alter the fact that sustained dialogue between the countries has been established.

---

[23] I am playing here with the title of Werner Sombart's analysis, at the start of the century, of Germany's geopolitical choice (*Händler und Helden* [München: Leipzig, 1915]).

[24] A. Milward, *The European Rescue of the Nation-State* (Berkeley: University of California Press, 1992); P. Anderson, "Under the Sign of the Interim" and "The Europe to Come," in *The Question of Europe*, ed. P. Gowan and P. Anderson (London: Verso, 1997); A. Moravcsik, *The Choice for Europe* (Ithaca: Cornell University Press, 1998).

This is no longer anarchy but a society of sorts, dominated by elites and with a good deal of nativist resentment coming from below, from those unable to swim in this larger sea. One should not exaggerate this achievement, as the crisis surrounding the euro makes clear. Still, there is diversity within Europe between different countries. But the situation within European societies is altogether less happy.

To begin with, we should remember that in 1914 something like sixty million people lived in states not ruled by their own "coculturals." Today there are very few examples of successful multinational regimes west of the Ukraine— Spain, for sure, idiosyncratic Switzerland as well, but with Britain and Belgium in the midst of fairly severe challenges. Much of the discussion of multiculturalism is in a sense hypocritical: we speak the language of tolerance now that we have no great national divisions to deal with. This is not to deny the bittersweet fact that democracy works more easily in most of Europe, including much of Central Europe and the Balkans, precisely because forced homogenization has taken place. Equally, it may well be the case that national homogeneity helps flexible economic adjustment. This seems to be true of Denmark, although the core of homogeneity was achieved in that country well before the twentieth century.[25] This does not for a moment justify or call for forced homogenization, not least as there are cases—Greece comes to mind—where its legacies remain toxic. And one should anyway be rather cautious in this whole area. It may well be that national homogeneity al-

[25] J. L. Campbell and J. A. Hall, "Defending the Gellnerian Premise: Denmark in Historical and Comparative Context," *Nations and Nationalism* 16 (2010).

lows for flexible adjustment, but the extent to which it encourages innovation is open to question.

More important is the marked failure of many European
countries to integrate into their social fabric the immigrants
that their low fertility rates make necessary. Such immigrants are physically present, very often wishing to belong,
but they remain excluded in the ways that count.[26] Housing
patterns and low marriage rates of immigrants into the host
community demonstrate this in the clearest manner possible. So too does the rise all over Europe of right-wing parties
directed at immigrants, which very often show particular
hostility to immigrants from Muslim countries. It is very noticeable that countries with a long history of national homogeneity—Denmark being a prime example—have especially
great difficulty in this regard. Recent legislation in that
country has a very particular character: it is leftist in wishing
to preserve high welfare benefits for Danes but right/na-
tionalist in wishing to deny such benefits to outsiders. It
would be idle, perhaps sad to say, to imagine multiculturalism in a country with such a homogeneous past, but the
worrying thing is the tacit refusal to allow those present to
move from their status as "new Danes" to becoming Danes.

There are some causes for optimism in Europe. Political
design has successes to its credit. It looks as if the complex
consociational agreements designed for Northern Ireland
will work. Ukraine is holding together precisely because
there is no attempt to homogenize the country in linguistic

[26] G. Schmidt and V. Jakobsen, *Pardannelse Blandt Etniske Minoriteter I Dan-
mark* (Copenhagen: Socialforskningsinstituttet, 2004); T. Shakoor and R. W.
Riis, *Tryghed Blandt Unge Nydanskere* (Copenhagen: Tryg Fonden, 2007).

terms.[27] Most Spaniards seem content with multiple identities, and it matters little, in any case, if Spain—or the United Kingdom or Belgium—were to dissolve, as long, that is, as the separable units could remain within the European Union. After all, this is a struggle over a single passport, a single European citizenship. But one should not exaggerate here. Consider Switzerland.[28] Here we do have the important example of a multiethnic nation, or, in an alternative formulation, a successful state-nation. But the fact that different ethnicities live together does not for a moment mean that the country as a whole is open to outsiders. Very much to the contrary, contemporary Swiss politics is as concerned to exclude outsiders as is that of Denmark.[29]

To summarize the argument, civil nationalism is profoundly to be desired, but it is also rather hard to achieve. It is interesting to discover that the United States is more of a pioneer in this regard than are European countries. But both these great areas of the North have at their respective hearts a good deal of background homogeneity. In conclusion, we *can* realistically hope that the non-European world may manage its affairs better by invention rather than by imitating the North. We have already seen that the ingenuity of the linguistic regime of India that allows this huge country to remain united. It is possible to have multiple

[27] In this context there is much to be said for distinguishing "national" from "holding together" federations, as explained by A. Stepan, J. Linz, and Y. Yadav, *Crafting State-Nations*.

[28] A. Wimmer, "A Swiss Anomaly? A Relational Account of National Boundary Making," *Nations and Nationalism* 17 (2011).

[29] A. Wimmer, *Nationalist Exclusion and Ethnic Conflict: Shadows of Modernity* (Cambridge: Cambridge University Press, 2002), chapter 8.

identities and to create consociational and federal arrangements that allow several nations to live within a single political frame. Also, the presence of a large number of ethnic groups, perhaps one hundred and twenty in Tanzania alone—none of which is near demographic dominance—can undermine homogenizing politics: multiethnic coalitions may be mandated, given that no group dares play the ethnic card. Of course, Africa has seen little sustained interstate war since decolonization, though it has been plagued by low-intensity internal strife—and by more recent resource-driven conflicts. A negative side of the absence of sustained geopolitical conflict has been relative failure in state-building.[30] But there is another, more positive side to the picture. One factor that intensified ethnic cleansing in Europe was competing claims to a single piece of territory. Near-absolute endorsement of the principle of nonintervention has meant that this factor has by and large been missing in Africa. Of course, none of this is to say, once again, that sweetness and light can be guaranteed.

---

[30] J. Herbst, *States and Power in Africa: Comparative Lessons in Authority and Control* (Princeton: Princeton University Press, 2000).

CHAPTER 5

Intelligence in States

International law is based upon this principle: that the various
nations ought to do, in peace, the most good to each other, and, in
war, the least harm possible, without detriment to their genuine
interests.

(Montesquieu, *L'Esprit des Lois*)

This chapter follows Montesquieu in suggesting the desirability and sociological importance of restraint and civility
in the most vicious arena of all: war between states. But the
citation is not mine. Rather, it stands as the legend to Raymond Aron's great *Peace and War*, and it is to his thought in
the arena of interstate behavior that this chapter is devoted.
It may be useful to say immediately that Aron strikes me as
the very model of a responsible intellectual (especially given
the contentions of chapter 7), a social philosopher of intellectual power and prudence who served his society with
great courage and considerable style. A few comments about
this are in order before describing and praising his remarkable contribution.

In retrospect, his achievement as a political columnist,
who habitually wrote an opinion piece once a week for more

than forty years, is quite extraordinary—and deeply revealing of his desire to educate a generation of the French elite
by drawing them away from the blocked politics of the
1930s toward the great years of national reconstruction that
followed the Second World War. Just as important was the
way in which he changed French intellectual life by criticiz-
ing both thinkers of the Right, especially in the war years
when writing for de Gaulle's *La France Libre*, and of the Left
for most of his career, the latter stand requiring exceptional
bravery.[1] So it makes sense to start by capturing something
of the flavor of the great French social scientist. Then it is
necessary to recall exactly what he said about the sociology
of states. Of course, he wrote a great deal, with some of his
interventions—for example, those on the force de frappe—
now being rather dated. But his central contentions were designed to be timeless. Of course, concern throughout is directed to asking whether the changed circumstances of our
time have upheld those central contentions. Is Aron's work
still useful? Does it even suggest new avenues of inquiry?

I met Aron on several occasions in the last years of his life.
On the occasion that I interviewed him, it became rapidly
apparent that he hated being asked personal questions.
Hence, the conversation changed its tempo and moved to
analysis of questions of political economy at the forefront of
public attention at the time. I had become convinced of the
importance of social contracts, that is, of the purportedly
beneficial effects of corporatist arrangements between state,

---

[1] T. Judt, *Past Imperfect: French Intellectuals, 1944–56* (Berkeley: University of
California Press, 1992).

capitalists, and workers in ensuring sufficient social peace to allow the economy to work effectively. The lack of such arrangements surely had something to do with the relative decline of Britain compared to its European neighbors. Aron understood this position, but began to probe. If one adopted this view and turned it into policy, what would be the consequences? Was it possible to have national corporatist policies in a world that was changing? Was corporatism a unitary affair in any case? Might I not be mixing up cooperative bargaining institutions with Keynesian policies—with the two not always going hand in hand? Might not corporatism lead to stalemate and stagnation in the longer run? Had it not perhaps worked well at a particular period, and in particular countries? The questions came thick and fast, but in a wholly courteous manner, prepared to accept that my position might be correct. But, of course, I had not thought through half of the questions that Aron raised. It was as if I was playing chess with someone who could see four or five moves further ahead in the game afoot. I left feeling rather foolish. Rereading Aron makes one aware, more than ever, both of his extraordinary intelligence and of his determination to comment only on the basis of genuine knowledge. He, too, had felt himself a fool on his return from Nazi Germany when, after unleashing a moral critique, he had been asked by Joseph Paganon, an undersecretary for foreign affairs, what course of action he recommended—and he had no reply. Spasms of self-admiring moral critique were self-indulgent pieces of political romanticism that were to be avoided at all costs. That experience led him to become a consequentialist, a follower of Max Weber in insisting that criticism was only responsible when one had a rigorous and practicable policy alternative to offer.[2]

We will see that the single most important element of his work on international relations was its insistence on the need for genuine thought. A very striking example can be given immediately. One of the most interesting commentaries on Aron's work in recent years has been that of Pierre Birnbaum in a remarkable book assessing the impact of a Jewish background on a series of social scientists.[3] Aron's astonishing bravery is clearly demonstrated in his decision to take a stand against the implicit anti-Semitism of de Gaulle's comments about Israel at the end of the Six-Day War, not least because this put in question, at least in the eyes of others, his own carefully described self-identity—as a Frenchman with a Jewish background. Of greater relevance here, though, is the astonishing clarity of his views toward Israel itself at this time. The first column that he wrote for *Figaro* after the end of the war, on July 12, 1967, suggested that the absolute nature of the victory meant that "Israel has not defeated the Arab States; by a lightning operation it has won a military success which will not be decisive politically."[4] His stand at this point is wholly in accord with the sentiment expressed by Montesquieu at the beginning of this chapter. It also reflects his analysis of the end of the Second World War, which strikingly criticized the policy of unconditional surrender

[2] R. Aron, *Mémoires: 50 ans de reflexion politique* (Paris: Julliard, 1983), 59.
[3] P. Birnbaum, *Geography of Hope*, chapter 4.
[4] R. Aron, *De Gaulle, Israel and the Jews* (London: Praeger, 1969), 63.

for increasing resistance to the Allies and allowing for greater Soviet expansion than was necessary.[5]

A second general comment about Aron, and one with particular relevance to his work on international relations, concerns the range and coherence of his social thought as a whole. On the one hand, all his work rests on a developed philosophical anthropology. It may be that his philosophical background, based as it was on an early encounter with Husserl, German neo-Kantians, and, above all, with Max Weber, was not the strongest part of his work. But he undeniably gained something from it; namely, the view that action was rational and that the job of the interpreter was to reconstruct as much as possible of the mental world of the actor. On the other hand, his intellectual stature in political economy and in the affairs of states allowed the insights of one field to challenge received theories in the other. There was no reason to believe that industrial society would bring peace.[6] Much more important than such Comtian illusions were Aron's varied works on imperialism, very often written with Marxist contentions at the back of his mind. Aron realized very quickly indeed that the core of capitalism very largely did not need the rest of the world, albeit our markets are often essential for less developed countries if they wish to prosper. Imperialism has marked all of human history: all that was really different in the nineteenth century is that the justification for such vaulting power had to be made in

---

[5] R. Aron, *Peace and War: A Theory of International Relations* (New York: Doubleday, 1966), 27–29.

[6] R. Aron, *La société industrielle et la guerre* (Paris: Plon, 1958).

economistic terms.[7] Aron once noted in an aside that acquaintance with large industrialists had been, so to speak, a disappointment in geopolitical terms: most great businessmen had no ideas in this realm, which was not surprising, as their concentration was on making money within rules to which they adapted. Probably one of his most decisive interventions in French political life is not known to English-speaking readers. France was deeply—and variously—split over its empire. The military was obsessed with its retention, as it felt Spain's loss of empire had led it into poverty. If the Right supported retention, the Left critiqued it very largely for moral reasons—objecting in forceful terms to the brutalities involved. Aron very likely shared these latter views, but his intervention had an entirely different character, wholly representative of its author.[8] If Algeria was to be considered an integral part of France, as those who wished to retain empire demanded, then certain consequences followed. The crucial one was simple: very large sums of money would have to be spent to raise the standard of living in North Africa so that it reached a level comparable with that in the metropole. In other words, empires had only been possible under low-intensity rule: anything more direct would mean that they would be so expensive as to lower the standard of living of those in Paris.

Finally, attention should be given to the claim made by one of Aron's closest associates to the effect that Aron's most substantial achievement was to produce a philosophy of history for our time, a guide orienting us to the constraints and

[7] R. Aron, *Imperialism and Colonialism* (Leeds: Leeds University Press, 1959).
[8] R. Aron, *La tragédie Algérienne* (Paris: Plon, 1958).

options available to us.[9] It is easy to see what is meant. *The Century of Total War* is a superlative example, as it describes the disasters that came to the European multipolar sphere, hitherto the center of human progress, once high technology was applied to state competition: it created total war that escaped, at least for a period, all forms of rational political control.[10] With hindsight surely few would disagree with the claim made in *Le Grande Schisme*, that there was something like a binary choice to be made between the Soviet and American spheres, and that basic liberalism dictated plumping for the latter.[11] Such an early and stark definition of the position of the West was exceptionally brave, while the permanent stress on Soviet hegemony as a form of imperialism made Aron much loved by the liberal opposition in the erstwhile socialist bloc. *The Great Debate* remains one of the most sophisticated discussions on the logic of nuclear exchanges, at once interpreting American theory for Europeans while pointing out flaws in that logic apparent to Europeans.[12] It is perhaps still more important to mention *The Imperial Republic*, a pathbreaking example of international political economy concerned with military power and economic strength, and more particularly with the seigniorage that was extracted as the result of primacy—a theme, one might add, that shows how very far Aron was from being a thinker of the Right, albeit he was often falsely classified as

[9] P. Hassner, "Raymond Aron and the History of the 20th Century," *International Studies Quarterly* 29 (1985).

[10] R. Aron, *The Century of Total War* (Garden City, NY: Doubleday, 1954).

[11] R. Aron, *Le Grand Schisme* (Paris: Gallimard, 1948).

[12] R. Aron, *The Great Debate: Theories of Nuclear Strategy* (Garden City, NY: Doubleday, 1964).

such.[13] One can easily add to the list: a continual line of thought noted that European unity was likely to be rather shallow, not least given the early failure of Europe to see to its own defense; the subtlety of Aron's argumentation about NATO's defenses; and the general account of the personal, class, and international relations of our time.[14] The fact that so many of Aron's books are replete with careful analyses of the political situations of the times in which he lived seems to me entirely honorable, a remarkable example of the political responsibility of an intellectual able and determined to improve the lot of his society. Some might like to add to this the suggestion that we are unlikely to discover many sociological laws, which makes analytic history—that is, history written with sociological categories to the fore—quite often all that can be achieved. But the key point is that in the end Aron did discover and emphasize central features of the world of states—to which we can now turn.

We must begin with what Aron insists upon as a starting point. He regards himself as a descendant of Thucydides, Machiavelli, and Hobbes (all of whom are cited on many occasions) in insisting that the international arena is wholly different from the national. Hobbes is right: while anarchy is prevented inside a country by the presence of a leviathan, the international realm sees countries arming themselves against each other in order to protect their own security. At

---

[13] R. Aron, *The Imperial Republic* (London: Weidenfeld, 1974).
[14] I have in mind these texts: *Plaidoyer pour l'Europe décadente* (Paris: Lafonte, 1977); "De l'impérialisme américain à la hégémonisme soviétique," *Commentaire* 2 (1979); *La Querelle de la CED* (Paris: A. Colin, 1956; coedited with D. Lerner); *Progress and Disillusion* (London: Pall Mall Press, 1969).

best, the international realm is, to use a Kantian expression to which we will return, that of an "asocial society." Such a view undermines the pretensions of a certain version of sociology—present among the later Durkheimians who had taught Aron—that imagines that the historical record can be explained wholly with reference to social variables. Aron insists that this is not so. The First World War was occasioned by normal interstate rivalries: no social development made it necessary, albeit an increase in industrial power certainly affected its duration. Moreover, if war can result merely from the calculations and miscalculations of statesmen, just as important is the fact that social developments can quite often result from geopolitical events. The logic of class structure was not able to explain the different class relations of East and West Germany during the Cold War (best described, as Aron properly insisted, as "la paix belliqueuse"): what mattered was that, as Stalin suggested would happen, the victor on each side imposed its own social system. All of this is to say that Aron owes a huge debt to basic realism. This is scarcely surprising. One place where one can see it early on is in his reaction to the Nazi-Soviet Pact.[15] He describes himself as stunned by the news, but only for a moment; he was able almost instantly to see the logic involved and aware that states might find very different ways of protecting themselves. Another much more general theme in his work is mild skepticism toward the view that state competition might come to an end through the spread of international law. It is important to note that he had nothing

[15] Aron, *Mémoires*, 161.

against this as an ideal. But his charge against those holding this view was simple: namely, that all too often they replaced analysis with hope. Just as important, the desire to escape war through law might well increase conflict:

> The morality of law is the antithesis of the morality of struggle, because the law is valid for all, without consideration of persons, whereas the promises made by states or by gangsters are essentially linked to persons. But since international law is conservative, since states have never fully accepted its obligations, since, further, no tribunal, judging in equity, recommends the necessary changes, the states that invoke the morality of law often pass for hypocrites rather than heroes. A rare event in itself, respect for the law is too readily explained by national interest. If acted upon more frequently, this same respect would multiply wars and make them inexpiable.[16]

The idealist forgets that order depends on the calculation of forces, the neglect of which is deemed to be irresponsible. One must calculate consequences, and means, within the structure of relations within which we live and move.

One can complement this last paragraph with one concerned with political science, and more particularly with the current condition of international relations theory. For it is an astonishing fact that realism has become something of a dirty word within that discipline, curiously displaced by the

---

[16] Aron, *Peace and War*, 609.

ending of the United States–Soviet rivalry. An outsider must see this as a form of madness. Realism is far from perfect, as some of the rest of this book will demonstrate. Nonetheless, it remains the case that the structure of the world polity has, to put it mildly, interstate rivalry at its core. A core realist maxim such as "the enemy of my enemy is my friend" continues to explain a very great deal, perhaps most obviously in Russian behavior under Putin in recent years. But Aron's contribution to the theory of international relations goes well beyond what can usefully be termed "simple" realism. The central claim here is that he offered us a sophisticated version of that basic approach, at once more complex and more meritorious. Two elements are involved: first, the pure logic of realism, and then, necessarily deriving from it, the sociological elements that Aron brought into realism, not to deny or to replace the basic insights of that theory but rather to improve it by better explaining both the escalation to extremes and the periods of diminished conflict that mark the historical record. Both elements combine to form not just a descriptive system but quite as much a prescriptive view as to how we should conduct ourselves. What is at issue is civility and prudence.

Simple realism can be defined as the view that states act at all times and under every regime, whatever their political character, so as to advance their national interests. Aron rejects this view. It is empty because it is tautological: whatever a state does can be defined after the event in these terms. The situation is very similar to that of a critic of utilitarianism who suggested that self-laceration was painful, only to receive the reply from Bentham himself that the actions involved must have been pleasurable to the person involved. The difficulty here is that a notion so flexible cannot offer us any guidance to the future. And just as important in Aron's case were his personal experiences, both of international affairs and of the intellectual developments of the interwar years. History felt as if it was speeding up, with events crowding each other out in a bewildering fashion. The conclusion that Aron drew from this was very straightforward: the aims of states might vary, with leaders sometimes choosing glory, at other times acting to realize an idea or simply enjoying the exercise of power.

> Security, power, glory, idea are essentially heterogeneous objectives which can be reduced to a single term only by distorting the human meaning of diplomatic-strategic action. If the rivalry of states is comparable to a game, what is "at stake" cannot be designated by a single concept, valid for all civilizations at all periods. Diplomacy is a game in which the players sometimes risk losing their lives, sometimes prefer victory itself to the advantages that would result from it.[17]

It is at this point that his philosophical anthropology becomes relevant. To understand human life, it was just as necessary for a statesman as for a sociologist to reconstruct the rationality of the social actors with whom one was involved. A particularly striking example of the disasters that could follow when this maxim was ignored was provided in Aron's

[17] Ibid., 91.

view by American behavior in Vietnam.[18] The American international relations profession had become excessively abstract, reductive in the worst sense by ignoring the complexities of reality in its insistence on a simplifying realism concerned only with levels of power. That profession had failed to realize that the stake involved was utterly different for the two sides—crucial for the North Vietnamese and of far less significance for the United States. This is a striking example of Aron's independence of mind, in this case that of a thinker who was both anticommunist and grateful for the actions of the United States in postwar Europe, but who was prepared nonetheless to produce one of the most stinging critiques of American policy ever written.

Aron's great book on Clausewitz, appropriately entitled *Penser la guerre, Clausewitz*, developed these thoughts still further.[19] Two arguments of the first volume of the book devoted to Clausewitz's system of thought deserve noting here. First, Aron makes much of Clausewitz's critique of various thinkers of his own time, especially that of Heinrich Dietrich von Bülow, which suggested that strategic thought could be turned into a science. The most crucial reason why this could never happen was that the field of strategy is necessarily open. One must guess at the other side's calculations and be aware that they are trying to guess your own. In these circumstances all that strategic training could offer was the

[18] R. Aron, "The Evolution of Modern Strategic Thought: Problems of Modern Strategy," *Adelphi Papers* 9 (1969).
[19] R. Aron, *Penser la guerre*, 2 vols. (Paris: Gallimard, 1976). A useful commentary on the text is B. Cooper, "Aron's Clausewitz," in *Political Reason in the Age of Ideology: Essays in Honor of Raymond Aron*, ed. D. J. Mahoney and B. P. Frost (New York: Transaction, 2007).

art of thinking—of awareness of historic examples in combination with realization that entirely new moves were possible at any moment in time. Second, and still more important, were the implications that Aron drew from his superb
analysis of the textual changes in *On War*. Clausewitz had
experienced the brilliance of Napoleon firsthand, and
clearly regarded him when he first started to write his book
as nothing less than the god of war. Accordingly, his very
first definition of war had much in common with, or was a
version of, simple realism: it stressed the nature of the duel,
and went on to say that this necessarily led to an escalation
to extremes as each side followed a logic, deemed inevitable,
that led only to the attempt to establish total victory over
one's opponent. Aron demonstrates effectively that it was
only at the very end of his life that Clausewitz was able to
offer a fully comprehensive, trinitarian definition of war—
and to insist that the book as a whole needed to be read in
the light of this definition.

> War, considered in its concrete totality, is composed of
> a strange trinity: the *original violence* of its element,
> the hatred and hostility that must be considered as a
> blind natural tendency; the *play of probabilities and
> chance* which make it a free activity of the soul; and
> the subordinate nature of a *political instrument* by
> which it belongs purely to the *understanding*. The first
> of these terms is related to the *people*; the second, to
> the military commander (*Feldherr*); and the third, to
> the *government*.[20]

[20] R. Aron, "Reason, Passion and Power in the Thought of Clausewitz," *Social
Research* 39 (1972): 607–8; emphasis in the original.

This complete definition of war led Clausewitz to change his mind. Napoleon was a great military leader, but he did not understand the purpose of war. His attempt to win everything eventually bred a countervailing alliance in which all his gains were lost. Clausewitz came to appreciate in contrast the greater understanding of Frederick the Great, who gained territory and men through a more cautious policy, switching sides as needed to gain diplomatic strength and never threatening all his neighbors at one time. This is an example of the proper logic of realism: calculating the purposes of war carefully and controlling them so that any gains made can be permanent. In the second volume of *Penser la guerre, Clausewitz*, Aron makes exactly the same points in connection with Bismarck's victories in 1870, albeit with a slight exception. Bismarck was well aware that too great a victory, the annexation of too much territory, would turn France into an implacable enemy, and accordingly sought to end the war quickly. But popular pressure in Germany made this impossible, which suggests that the conduct of foreign policy, once the people are aroused, can be extremely difficult for statesmen. At this point it is very important to pause for a moment so as to avoid misunderstanding. The proper logic of realism should not be interpreted as a call for passivity, for limitation at all times. On the contrary, early, preemptive action can make most sense on occasions, not least in limiting deaths that might otherwise follow. What really matters is thought, working through the consequences of military action. Aron offended many in his lifetime by trying to work through the consequences of nuclear war on the grounds that this might do more to control the situation than simply hoping for the best.

This is also a good moment to pause and suggest that
Aron's thought remains supremely relevant in contemporary circumstances. Let us consider the most recent American intervention in Iraq. We now know enough to see that
the urge for war is best interpreted in terms of Aron's insistence on varied motivation. There is little sign, at least given
the evidence before us so far, that war was contemplated for
economic reasons, as so many believe. Rather, there seems to
have been a personal desire of the younger Bush to complete
the work of his father. More important though was a generalized sense of unlimited power joined with the political romanticism of a set of intellectuals who were convinced that
they could bring democracy to the Middle East. The most
important thing to bear in mind is simply that hubris joined
to an idea prevented sufficient consequentialist thought.
This was most obviously so in terms of the lack of planning
to deal with the situation that would result from victory—
or, more precisely, the lack of a well-developed "Plan B"
should the expectations, anyway naive, of being welcomed
immediately by all groups with open arms prove to be incor-
rect. But the lack of thought was much more general and
much more dangerous. The United States has not attacked a
country that possesses nuclear weapons, and very probably
will never do so. Hence, the real drive for Iran to have such
weapons is simply the desire to avoid the fate that befell its
neighbor. This is not for a moment to say that a war to top-
ple Saddam Hussein was necessarily wrong. A war with
large-scale diplomatic backing, seen by the world as less arbitrary, might have succeeded better, both in itself and in
not threatening Iran to the same extent. However, the gen-

eral point is clear: American strategists were the most simple of realists and failed to act intelligently.

Perhaps the most familiar criticism of realism is that it reifies the state. The international system is sometimes seen in terms of a billiard table, with each state like a ball that is necessarily involved in a logic of collision and reaction. Realism exemplifies much of social science. This is true, for example, of the concept of the state quite generally, which is habitually defined as an institution capable of monopolizing the means of violence within a particular territory. The point to be made against this is that "stateness" is an aspiration as much as a reality. This most certainly applies to the means of violence in many contemporary states that are recognized as such by the international community. But it applies quite as much to other social forces that escape the caging that gives states their power. For instance, increasing economic interchange has made it harder for states to control economic processes. One could, in fact, go somewhat further and say that it is only in the rarest of circumstances that states have achieved their desire: that of being complete power containers. Differently put, states normally have to learn to live within the larger societies of economic and military competition. Aron's work in international relations gains much of its sophistication from realizing this very basic point. It allows him to make the two forceful sociological contributions that are at the heart of *Peace and War*.

The first of these surely derives from his historical experience. There is an enormous difference between states that live within a relatively homogeneous world and the heterogeneity that results from the presence of states seeking to overturn the rules of an established international order. Homogeneity can usefully be seen in Kantian terms, as an asocial or semisocialized world. Understanding between states is likely to be high when elements of an international society are present. The conduct of foreign policy in the eighteenth century was surely helped by the fact that diplomacy was habitually conducted in a single language by members of the same aristocratic and dynastic order. Equally, the fact that Bismarck and Lord Salisbury used the same maps aided understanding. In the postwar period, the United States took great care to socialize the elites of countries under its purview, while the fear of mutual nuclear catastrophe soon produced something of a common elite culture between the Soviet Union and the United States—the "enemy partners," as Aron liked to describe them. The contrast to all this is obvious. The ideological explosions of the Wars of Religion, the French Revolutionary Wars, and the revolutionary forces of Nazism and (the early years of) Bolshevism went hand in hand with an escalation to extremes. One obvious reason for this was simply the desire of a revolutionary force to mold the world in its own image. Just as important was the inability of traditional regimes to understand revolutionary forces, which thereby drove those forces to extremes, in a game of mirrors that pushed conflict to extremes. Importantly, lack of understanding often continued even when revolutionary forces had lost their bite. It took a long time, for example, to realize that the Soviet Union lost its revolutionary zeal rather quickly after 1917, with its behavior thereafter being explicable in standard realist terms.

Second, Aron made the most of the need to make states

intelligent. This can be particularly clearly seen in the last chapter of the second volume of *Penser la guerre, Clausewitz*, which considered various means designed to bring peace. Aron had little time for the Maoist view that the extension of class struggle would bring peace, for he felt it all too likely that socialist states would arm against each other. But he was well aware that states were not necessarily good at calculating. For one thing, they might lack capacity, as was the case in the early period of the recent American intervention in Iraq, when only a handful of people spoke the languages necessary to establish any understanding of popular feelings. For another, statesmen needed to be trained to exercise judgment so as to become aware of the iterative nature of the relations between states so that the limited norms of international society could, in the absence of revolutionary forces, be cemented and perhaps even spread.

At best, rational states can work within a homogeneous world. But whenever two elements are present, one wishes to know which one has the most importance. The intelligence of the state matters most for Aron, for it is indispensable both in homogeneous and heterogeneous international orders. The state alone has the capacity to provide us with a way of life, and Aron's loyalty to this principle, established in his earliest years, marks all his thought.[21]

Regrettably, Aron's work on international relations has not, I think, had a direct influence on most sociologists. Thus, it is ironic to see that his central insights are being rediscovered by a new generation, driven to his conclusions

---

[21] R. Aron, "De l'objection de conscience," *Revue de Metaphysique et de Morale* 41 (1934).

124   Chapter 5

through powerful empirical work. The most striking example is the work of Michael Mann, the leading comparative historical sociologist of this generation. International politics has always been at the center of Mann's work, most strikingly in his account of one of Aron's own favorite topics—that of the origins of the First World War.[22] What is noticeable about Mann's account is that it stresses the two sociological factors just identified and pays particular attention to the lack of rationality on the part of the German state in terms of its regime structure—roughly speaking, in terms of that state being a court more than an agency that allowed the setting of priorities. A rather similar argument about the origins of the First World War has been offered by Jack Snyder in an impressive book that seeks to generalize about the relationship between types of state and the incidence of war and peace.[23] Snyder suggests that control of the state is likely to be high, with priority setting thereby possible when either a traditional elite or a single party is in control: in contrast, a semimobilized state with an authoritarian elite that feels threatened by nascent forces of democracy is likely to "bandwagon," to offer something to every group in a way that undermines rational calculation.

This suggests a final thought. Aron was fond of saying that he had managed to hold on to hope even though his illusions had been dispelled. His theory of international rela-

[22] M. Mann, *The Sources of Social Power*, vol. 2, *The Rise of Classes and Nation-States, 1760–1914* (Cambridge: Cambridge University Press, 1993), chapter 21.
[23] J. Snyder, *Myths of Empire: Domestic Politics and International Ambitions* (Ithaca: Cornell University Press, 1993).

tions offers us a better way. But that it remains realist, always aware of novelty and of human folly, can be seen by noting just one counterexample to Snyder's fine book. Hitler was in control of his state yet ravaged Europe in the middle of the last century. One can have total control over one's state yet still bring destruction to one's society.[24]

[24] J. A. Hall, *International Orders* (Cambridge: Cambridge University Press, 1996).

PART TWO

ENEMIES

CHAPTER 6

Down with Authenticity

No cultural turn is so archetypically modern as the insistence that one behave in an authentic manner. The prophet and great exemplar of this view is Rousseau, whose *Confessions* sought approval precisely because the shocking revelations therein laid his soul bare. Of course, the book did not reveal the truth, at least obviously or in the round. One of the strangest elements in cultural life is the way in which art can prefigure later realities, and I have always found a resemblance between Rousseau and Alceste, the proponent of authenticity in Molière's *The Misanthrope*. The point of the play is that this putatively authentic character is in fact the only one who is self-deceived. This is a useful introduction here, for it raises skepticism toward the cultural turn in question. A still better guide to what follows can be found in an aphorism of Ernest Gellner's commenting on Polonius's advice to be true to oneself: " 'Know Thyself'—an absurdity, presupposing a given, determinate self."[1] These citations, the title of the chapter, and its placement in this part of the book make my own hostility to the demand for authenticity obvious. The intent is that of explaining why the

[1] The aphorism was not published, but it is cited in J. A. Hall, *Ernest Gellner: An Intellectual Biography* (London: Verso, 2010), 76.

demand for authenticity is so meretricious, so much opposed to civility. Doing so will not just cast light on the
composite definition of civility already offered but will spell
out certain key presuppositions upon which that definition
rests.

The best way in which we can gain purchase on the call
for authenticity is to consider the work of Erving Goffman.
His work is celebrated, but it is difficult to interpret. The
difficulty does not lie in the detail that he provided about
daily life, most of which is highly suggestive, but in the lack
of a set of generalizations on which to hang his description
of the minutiae of social interaction. For example, it is fair
to say that Goffman had no single theory of the self, despite
titles such as *The Presentation of the Self in Everyday Life*.
The diffidence toward theorizing was perhaps a tribute to
the complexities of social life, but this served him badly, for
relative silence on his part has not prevented others, quite
naturally, from attempting to place his work. The argument
of this chapter is that the main interpretation of his work on
offer is negative, and that this is both misinformed and sociologically naive.

The main interpretation here is considered to be that either derived from or at least epitomized by Alvin Gouldner's *The Coming Crisis of Western Sociology*—something of
a classic in its time that is now suffering from the neglect
that followed the success of its attack on Talcott Parsons.[2]

---

[2] A. Gouldner, *The Coming Crisis of Western Sociology* (New York: Basic Books,
1979). Cf. R. Sennett, "Two on the Aisle," *New York Review of Books*, November
1, 1971; J. O'Neill, *Sociology as a Skin Trade* (London: Heinemann, 1972);
C. Bryant, "Privacy, Privatisation and Self-Determination," in *Privacy*, ed.

Gouldner's argument was that Goffman's "impression managers" are Machiavellian manipulators of an especially nasty type. This type of personality does not represent human nature as such but rather the status-conscious, anxiety-ridden world of the middle class in late capitalist society—a character type sometimes explicitly identified with the "other-directed" personality made famous by David Riesman's *The Lonely Crowd*. Still more important are the moral and political consequences that are held to follow. Goffman's work is judged to be politically suspect, if not downright conservative, since he treats the ground rules of "public order" on which impression management relies as if they were natural rather than the product of a social pathology. In contrast, the critics recommend that we learn to trust each other openly so as to create a "sincere" society—by which they mean, as we shall see, a society based on authenticity. Gouldner makes the point with force. He follows a long quotation, appropriately from Rousseau, with this injunction:

> This passionate demand for artless "sincerity," and this moral outrage at the constraint that custom imposes on the baring of the heart, is rooted in the assumption that man is at bottom good and he therefore need not fear self-exposure or the possibility that he would be less than he should be if he trusted his own impulses.[3]

J. Young (Chichester: John Wiley and Sons, 1978); I. Craib, *Existentialism and Sociology* (Cambridge: Cambridge University Press, 1976); A. Dawe, "The Underworld View of Erving Goffman," *British Journal of Sociology* 24 (1973).

[3] Gouldner, *The Coming Crisis*, 386–87.

A point that is close to this must also be mentioned. One critic within this school has argued that the practices described by Goffman are a danger to democracy; they are seen—within a framework derived from Ralf Dahrendorf's account of *Society and Democracy in Germany*—as representing a retreat into privacy at the expense of those public virtues on which democratic order depends.[4] One might add that in this, as in other cases, a disapproval of Goffman's subjects merges easily into a disapproval of Goffman for studying them.

The views of these critics can usefully be termed "existentialist," for they believe that human beings are possessors of a "real" self; all stress the potential of human beings as free and creative actors. However, they are aware that the full and proper development of the real self does not always occur. The early Sartre argued that the individual at times hides from full freedom, seeking to escape the responsibility for existence in "bad faith"—the latter condition consisting in the futile pretense of being a passive and determined object. The existentialist critics considered here owe most, however, to the later Sartre, who came to blame the particular organization of Western society instead of life as such for these vain and sorry attempts to shrug off one's freedom. But despite this change Sartre was never really able to escape his pessimistic belief that there is no guaranteed route to "good faith" consisting in the respect of one's own self and that of others.[5] The existentialist critics considered here do

[4] C.G.A. Bryant, "Privacy, Privatisation and Self-Determination," in *Privacy*, ed. J. Young.
[5] R. Aron, *History and the Dialectics of Violence* (Oxford: Oxford University Press, 1970).

not share his pessimism, and are in fact aglow with human potency. They imagine that sincerity and open respect for one's own and another's self is possible. Far richer concepts of self and sociability are held to be necessary to do justice to our condition and potential.

The best place to begin to untangle these issues is through an examination of the thought, and the political consequences of the thought, of Rousseau and his great descendant Sartre. They are relevant here since it is their conception of the real self openly embraced that underlies the ideas of the existentialist critics. Both begin their political philosophies from a radically individualist viewpoint that asserts the total freedom of human beings. Society is wholly absent from their initial deliberations; for any sociologist this tends to make what follows slightly naive and rather facile in that freedom is to be found in the fact that we feel free! However, if we suspend our disbelief, we find that such initial presuppositions lead to the development of political theories that are certainly authoritarian and clearly inimical to human freedom.

Political order becomes necessary for Rousseau and Sartre because there is "a problem of being." For all their vaunted belief in human freedom, both find that being—or, more simply, one's real self or individuality—is weak and desperately in need of social support. We need a sense of belonging. This is rather surprising. The burden of *Being and Nothingness* is to suggest that the social is a perpetual source of alienation; the gaze of the other is capable of turning a human being into an object. It was this that led Sartre to summarize his position in the famous observation that "hell is other people." Much the same degree of hatred of social life is to be

found in Rousseau. He felt, for example, that attending the
theater would detract from the settled and complete individuality of human beings since it would encourage such vi-
carious living secondhand that it would lead to dissatisfaction with one's own life.[6] Nevertheless, where others with the
same view of our condition suggest that we try to escape social life, Rousseau and Sartre attempt to found a political
theory.[7] Such a theory is not to have the negative task of al-
locating a private sphere protected by legal rights within
which the individual can do as he or she chooses. Instead the
theory's positive purpose is to ensure that everyone is conscious of and lives up to his true being at all times. The truth
to one's being, to one's real self is what Goffman's critics have
in mind when they recommend sincerity—by which they really mean, as noted, authenticity.

This attempt to square the circle of pure freedom and social order has, of course, been argued about endlessly; in my
opinion, for reasons to be noted later, the attempt either
fails or ends up supporting an extremely authoritarian political order. Both Rousseau and Sartre, when discussing
their ideal images of society, wish to anchor their political
order at a set moment. In Rousseau's case this occurs when
the social contract is established and the rights of individu-

[6] Rousseau made this argument in response to D'Alembert's claim that Geneva
needed a theater (J. J. Rousseau, *Letter to D'Alembert and Other Writings on the
Theater* [(1758) Hanover: University Press of New England, 2004]). The significance of this text was recognized by Lionel Trilling, *Sincerity and Authenticity*
(Oxford: Oxford University Press, 1974).
[7] This statement is slightly inaccurate. Rousseau was well aware of the attractions
of disentanglement, and is best interpreted as torn between the desire for con-
nectedness and the longing to be solitary.

als are ceded to the general will. For Sartre a similar moment occurs when the alienated "series" becomes a "group in fusion," in which all are joined in a common purpose, that of fighting against the oppressor. The tone of Sartre's example does not detract from the fact that the problem he wishes to solve is that of "grounding being," that is, giving support to human individuality. How these moments occur—how the social contract can be formed without the presence of the new men it is supposed to create, and how original freedom was lost—remains, despite commentators, a mystery. But more important is the consequence.

In Rousseau's case this is hard to establish precisely. If the general will acts on the votes of a mere majority, then it can no longer be general and legitimate; but if it does not act in this manner, then it is surely impotent; and Rousseau has not solved—at least in logic—the problem of founding a just political order. In Sartre's case, in comparison, everything is brutally clear. When the group forms it must be cemented by a vow; any member who abandons the very strenuous liberty Sartre has in mind automatically becomes a traitor who can and should be killed. A legitimate society has been founded, but it is one that is no longer based on possessing the actual consent of its citizens at any particular moment. The politics of total freedom, with its merging of public and private, ends in securing social cohesion through terror.

All of this is miles away from the social interactions described by Goffman. In order to understand it, we need to extract and highlight two important and rather different conceptions of the self contained within his work as a whole.

It may well be that the richness of his work would allow for further conceptions of the self to be discovered, but these two conceptions matter most, for they contrast most strikingly with the view put forward by his critics.

Throughout his work individuals are seen as making out as best they may within the context of social institutions that they did little to create. The self is portrayed as acted upon and as actively responding to such treatment. Thus "The Moral Career of a Mental Patient" shows the self the institution wishes to create, while "The Underlife of Public Institutions" shows the inmates "making out"—with the two essays being part of a single volume, *Asylums*.[8] But the distinction I wish to draw here between social self and personal self covers slightly different ground from that concerned with the self as product and as agent. I am concerned rather with what Goffman's sociology tells us about sincerity and the implications to be drawn from this.

We can approach an understanding of the social self through examining the one clear misreading of Goffman's work by his existentialist critics—namely, that the individuals he portrays are sinister manipulators. This is only the smallest element of Goffman's model of social interaction. In his first book he explicitly noted that

> most of these defensive techniques of impression management have a counterpart in the tactful tendency of the audience and outsiders to act in a protective way in order to help the performers save their own show.[9]

[8] E. Goffman, *Asylums* (London: Penguin, 1968).
[9] E. Goffman, *The Presentation of the Self in Everyday Life* (New York: Doubleday Anchor, 1959), 229.

It is tact and circumspection that allows interaction to occur at all. At moments of embarrassment capable of destroying the frame of reference that allows an interaction to occur, Goffman notes that "face-work," whether in the form of giving an excuse or of the mutual ignoring of a faux pas, can be undertaken to remedy the situation.[10] Crucially, such face-work will be undertaken both by the offender and by those offended. These points are summed up in this manner:

> Much of the activity occurring during an encounter can be understood as an effort on everyone's part to get through the occasion and all the unanticipated and unintentional events that can cast participants in an undesirable light, without disrupting the relationships of the participants. And if relationships are in the process of change, the object will be to bring the encounter to a satisfactory close without altering the expected course of development.[11]

In other words, Goffman's portrayal is less of a competitive set of liars and much more of a rather altruistic mutual aid society whose members help one another to get over difficult moments.

When we ask why people are so kind and tactful, we come to the core of the social self. Goffman's work, despite being included in readers concerned with symbolic interactionism, descends from Durkheim. It is well known that the great French sociologist believed that the "cult of the indi-

---

[10] E. Goffman, "On Face-Work," in his *Interaction Ritual* (London: Allen Lane, 1967).
[11] Ibid., 41.

vidual" had in part taken over—and should take over completely—from religion as the moral principle suitable for a differentiated society. Durkheim's own work was designed to extend a version of this respect so that the individual would be fully integrated within modern society.[12] Goffman's work in a sense begins where Durkheim's ends. He accepts that individualism is the central morality of our time, but goes beyond Durkheim in seeing how the sacred quality of the individual is created and maintained in everyday life. The practices that are involved in the ceremonial affirmation of the individual's sacredness—above all, those concerning deference and demeanor—do not concern us here. But two general points are in order. First, Goffman insists that these practices are social and have little to do with questions of personal individuality: "It may well be true that the individual has a unique self all his own," he notes disarmingly, but "evidence of [such a unique self] is thoroughly a product of joint ceremonial labour."[13] Second, Goffman suggests that it is in small-scale interactions within society that the larger moral order is affirmed. Rousseau wished us to affirm the values of the society in public and on a large scale; it is for this reason that he pays so much attention to the exercise of the general will. However, as Rousseau himself admitted, a large and complex society is unlikely to be able to have frequent communal re-endorsements. Hence, the rituals of daily life, in which the central moral value of

---

[12] Durkheim's views are made especially clear in his 1898 essay "Individualism and the Intellectuals," *Political Studies* 17 (1969). Goffman himself draws attention to the link to Durkheim in his "On the Nature of Deference and Demeanour," in *Interaction Ritual*.

[13] Goffman, "On the Nature of Deference and Demeanour," 85.

the larger society—namely, individualism—is affirmed, become extremely important for the ordering and symbolic integration of the society.

With this conception of the social self in mind, we can return to the question of sincerity. Goffman notes that

> those who are felt to be insincere or affected give the impression they are only concerned with what they can achieve in what is to follow and are willing to put on an act in order to achieve it. When the individual senses that others are insincere or affected he tends to feel they have taken unfair advantage of their communication position to promote their own interest; he feels they have broken the ground rules of interaction.[14]

This conception of insincerity is close to that which the existentialist critics have in mind when they criticize Goffman himself; it is amusing that his analysis of interaction shows that socially insincerity is also condemned. However, in one sense the critics are correct in detecting a difference between their position and the sincerity that can be derived from Goffman's observations. The existentialists are in favor of sincerity (hereafter always called authenticity in contrast to the social practice of sincerity—or, more accurately, civility—that we can derive from Goffman) in the sense of being true to oneself at all costs; their argument is essentially an antisocial one that would be summed up as "put yourself above social practices." Goffman's con-

14 Ibid., 90.

ception of the respect due to the social self leads to rather different recommendations. Goffman notes, for example, that one tends to greet and leave friends with a ritual designed to show that one takes relationships seriously.[15] In the short term such rituals are exaggerated, having little to do with the way in which the actors involved may be feeling. In the long term such tact seems less hypocritical since it can be seen as being true to the higher value of offering moral respect for individualism.

At this point we can say that the issue between Goffman and his critics is clear, and we will argue later, as noted, that there is a great deal more to recommend the sincerity or civility of Goffman's model than the authenticity of the existentialist. However, before examining the second conception of the self, an irony may be noted. The practices that Goffman describes arose from a respect for individualism. Yet it is those practices that are now held—and have been so held by writers as diverse as Tocqueville and Chesterton (a historical point arguing against the view that impression-management is a product of late capitalism society)—to threaten one's true self. Hence, we reach the ridiculous position that the existentialist critics wish to design new ways of encouraging individualism in the face of evidence, which they accept, that previous practices militate against such individualism. For the sake of clarity, it is well to anticipate a different way of reacting to this evidence, such as it is. It will be argued that the fear of excessive sincerity or civility as a political danger is vastly exaggerated, and that it is conse-

---

[15] Such practices are termed "access rituals" in his *Relations in Public* (London: Allen Lane, 1972), 107–10.

quently better not to seek to make politics a sphere of authenticity at all. Rather, we might leave the uniqueness that we are all apparently so happily endowed with to look after itself. This skeptical conclusion may well become clearer by examining the second conception of the self that concerns us here. Goffman offers us mere hints of this conception of the self; to understand its implications we must build upon his work.

One frequently gets the impression that some of the practices that Goffman describes are designed not just to give ritual backing to the sacred quality of the self but simply as a means by which the individual can get through the daily round with the minimum of interference with his personal self. This is especially true of relations in the large American city; here individuals seek to appear nonthreatening to each other so that the vulnerabilities they are exposed to by urban life do not become all engrossing.[16] A negative example of the same point is present in *Asylums*. Total institutions are able to destroy the two facts that give the individual a meaningful sense of freedom: the ability to control personal information and the right to choose to separate the audiences before whom separate roles are performed.[17] In both cases Goffman points to some sort of volition lying behind different "fronts," and it is that which is here termed "the personal self."

Goffman is unwilling to characterize this personal self for two particular reasons. First, his vision of society is, in Weberian terms, extremely disenchanted. The smallest minu-

[16] Ibid., 322.
[17] Goffman, "On the Characteristics of Total Institutions," in *Asylums*.

tiae of social life are subject to patterning according to Goffman. He is thus one of the few sociologists to study small-
scale interaction who is not seeking to celebrate a sense of
human creativity as a result. It is important to make this
point, given that theorists opposed to all notions of "social
determinism" cite his work to support their position. At the
conclusion of an essay on "Role Distance" Goffman explicitly notes that this phenomenon is "almost as subject to role
analysis as are the core tasks of sociology themselves"—a
statement made particularly striking by the fact that it is this
essay that is often cited by those who see an escape from social determinism in his work.[18] Second, however, Goffman's
work points to the extreme difficulty of knowing very much
about questions of self, both of others' and one's own—since
it is always hard to tell whether they are reacting to your pre-
sentations honestly. The latter is important in that inaccurate feedback may well lead to illusions about oneself.[19]

When these two points are taken in conjunction with the
idea that we have different fronts for different audiences, one
begins to note an uncanny resemblance between Goffman's
world and that of Marcel Proust. The introduction of the
novelist is designed to make it possible to turn these slightly
disconnected observations of Goffman into a fully fledged
theory of the personal self. Marcel, the hero of Proust's *À la
recherche du temps perdu*, finds his identity and that of others

[18] E. Goffman, "Role Distance," in his *Encounters* (London: Allen Lane, 1972).
The sociologist seeking to escape social determinism is Peter Berger, *Invitation to
Sociology* (New York: Anchor, 1963), 135–36.
[19] This aspect of Goffman's work is seen in his book dealing with spies and strategies, *Strategic Interaction* (Oxford: Basil Blackwell, 1972).

extremely hard to establish. On the one hand, he romanticizes love and "Society," but finds that knowledge brings disillusion; on the other hand, he finds it almost impossible to tell when people are lying to him. The novel is a success story in that Marcel does, in old age and after a great deal of personal suffering, establish his own identity. Whereas before he has suffered from "the intermittences of the heart"—has been, in other words, a succession of roles and experiences without a firm, integrating core—he becomes able to join all his experience within a common framework.

The conception of the personal self as something achieved is in diametric opposition to the ontological self, so evident in the work of Sartre. Whereas the latter glibly insists that we have a real self available at every moment of our lives, thereby making our attempts at living in bad faith necessarily doomed, Proust suggests that we must search hard for a self that we can truly call our own. For clarity's sake, it may be said that Proust believes that we can achieve an identity of our own after struggling to understand our past and the forces around us; he demonstrates the extreme difficulty of such a search, and guarantees no successful outcome. Surely, the belief that we have to try hard to understand ourselves corresponds more accurately to our condition than Sartre's facile insistence that we possess a real self at all times.

I can now make the central argument that follows on the basis of the analyses made up to this point. What is important is the relationship between the sincerity or civility of the social self and the identity that the personal self may be able to achieve. Bluntly, the practices of the social self will be seen as necessary to allow the identity of the per-

sonal self to be created. In other words, I wish to defend the paradox that lies at the heart of Proust's novel—that because the self is usually intermittent, moral ground rules are more necessary.[20] A series of points suggest that we favor civility above the authenticity endorsed by those who have criticized Goffman.

The first point is trivial, and certainly one not likely to convince an existentialist. It is an argument in favor of laziness. Sartre is a puritanical thinker who insists that we can never escape from consciousness, and should not try to do so. Proust's attitude is different, and this despite one remarkable coincidence in viewpoint.[21] He argues that habit—"bad faith" in Sartrean terms—is a human comfort; though he believes that artists should escape from habit, he does not suggest that they do so all the time. Further, Proust constantly notes that knowledge of oneself and of one's art comes when one is not prepared for it. Such knowledge cannot be ordered at will. Proust was an extreme rationalist, but he also realized the importance of, and wished to allow for, less serious parts of the human mind—above all, play—to come into effect.

A second consideration is perhaps as unlikely to convince a dedicated existentialist critic. In the face of crime in the American city, Goffman is held—notably in "Normal Appearances" in *Relations in Public*—to have become more pessimistic and conservative. In these circumstances, one critic holds Goffman to have favored ever more insistently

[20] This paradox was clearly recognized by M. Hindus, *The Proustian Vision* (New York: Columbia University Press, 1954), especially in the chapter "Ethics."
[21] I have in mind their pessimistic views on the self-defeating quality of love.

the maintenance of ground rules of public order, a move that is held to have placed him "on the side of the system."[22]

Much is wrong with this critique. First, Goffman is effectively found guilty by association. The fact that he is in favor of a set of rules is used to suggest that he endorses the rules currently operating in American society. This ignores Goffman's own assertion that "mutual dealings . . . could probably be sustained with fewer rules or different ones."[23] Second, it is worth remembering his analysis of "total institutions" in his classic *Asylums*. This is best read as an appeal for "the people" against a practice of late capitalist industrial society; and surely it is a novel and powerful appeal since it does not support the fashionable case that we do not need ground rules but argues instead for the less fashionable one that insists that it is inhumane to deprive anyone of the benefits—rights to privacy and information control—of such rules. Third, one discerns an extraordinarily antisociological assumption at work in this particular criticism. Social rules are well-nigh automatically equated with repression of the individual. Goffman, on the contrary, suggests that "persons *can* come together and voluntarily agree to abide by certain ground rules . . . the better to free attention from unimportant matters and get on with the business at hand."[24] This argument is Durkheimian in its implication that society is enabling, that without it we would be, for instance, incapable of communication given that language itself is social—a point made with

[22] Dawe, "The Underworld View," 251.

[23] Goffman, *Relations in Public*, 15.

[24] Ibid., 16; emphasis in original.

enormous power by François Truffaut in his film *L'Enfant
sauvage*.[25] Moreover, the belief that the absence of ground
rules would encourage us to approach each other with
warmth and spontaneity is illusory. Goffman is surely right
to show starkly the distrust and lack of warmth such a situation would breed. He thus escapes the simplistic "pro-
rules equals anti-people" charge. He is indeed in favor of
some rules, since without them the "truly human sociability and 'co-mingling'" the critic in question desires would
be impossible to attain.[26]

The third consideration matters more, not least because
Goffman makes it himself. He defended himself from the
charge of being politically suspect on the grounds that "he
who would combat false consciousness and awaken people
to their true interest has much to do, because the sleep is
very deep."[27] One example of such sleep may be drawn from
Stigma, given special interest by the fact that existentialism
is here considered directly.

The thesis of the book is straightforward. Goffman pictures the stigmatized person occupying an invidious position, full of personal strain. Stigmatized people consider
themselves to be normal yet know that the "normal" are un-
easy in their presence. One form of advice given to the stigmatized derives from existentialism in general, and more
particularly from Sartre's *Anti-Semite and Jew*. The advice
consists of Sartre's habitual insistence that one should be au-

---

[25] Truffaut came from a poor background, and the praise of society has real teeth
in consequence, as it can be read as a critique of the wilder fantasies of May 1968.

[26] Dawe, "The Underworld View," 253.

[27] E. Goffman, *Frame Analysis* (Harmondsworth: Penguin, 1975), 14.

thentic. The benefits of Goffman's humanity and of his skeptical way of dealing with cant are clearly seen in his analysis of this piece of advice. He suggests that the one thing, say, a disabled person does not wish to be told is to be authentic since this means in practical terms recognizing himself as less than normal. He notes rather acidly that

> the shrewdest position for him to take is . . . one which has a false bottom; for in many cases the degree to which normals accept the stigmatised individual can be maximized by his acting with full spontaneity and naturalness as if the conditional acceptance of him, which he is careful not to overreach, is full acceptance.[28]

A fourth consideration concerns directly political matters. One claim of the critics, as noted, was that the world he describes is unhealthy because it exalts private above public virtues, which are held to be dangerous given Dahrendorf's account of the social roots of Nazism. But this is a misuse of Dahrendorf. For the German sociologist distinguishes between public virtues as "a model of general intercourse between men" and private virtues "which provide the individual with standards for his own perfection, which is conceived as being devoid of society."[29] He suggests that the motto of the former might be "keep smiling" and of the latter "be

---

[28] E. Goffman, *Stigma: Notes on the Management of Spoiled Identity* (Englewood Cliffs, NJ: Prentice-Hall, 1963), 122–23.

[29] R. Dahrendorf, *Society and Democracy in Germany* (New York: Anchor Books, 1969), 286.

truthful." What this amounts to is quite clear: Dahrendorf is in favor of politics based on civility rather than a concern for authenticity.

There are a number of reasons why authenticity should be kept out of politics, why politics should not be personalized. It has already been suggested that theories with the best intentions end up with authoritarian conclusions when trying to create political order based on respect for authenticity. The practical precedents are, of course, much worse: the most famous example of a politician basing his legitimacy on a claim of personal authenticity is that of Adolf Hitler.[30] And while it would be ridiculous to accuse Sartre of somehow supporting a single authentic individual, it is nevertheless worrying that the colonizers he condemns are treated as totally inauthentic and consequently less than human.[31] Finally, we may remember that Riesman has argued that "this focus on sincerity, both in popular culture and in politics, leads the audience tolerantly to overlook the incompetence of the performers."[32]

Dahrendorf sees no link at all between other-directed and totalitarian politics:

> Men who are trying to get on with one another are probably spared the extreme evilness that makes it possible simply to rule some people out of the world

---

[30] See the brilliant opening chapters of J. P. Stern, *Hitler, the Führer and the People* (London: Fontana, 1975). Equally striking was Günter Grass's assault on Heideggerian language by having a character use it when speaking of concentration camps in *Dog Years* (New York: Harcourt, Brace and World, 1965).

[31] Aron, *History and the Dialectics of Violence*, 105.

[32] Riesman, *The Lonely Crowd*, 194.

of men in order to expedite them out of it afterwards.[33]

This is not to say that he considers other-direction something to be ignored. He agrees with Riesman, however, that the answer to this lies in reinforcing respect for privacy as a separate realm.[34] And again, it is important to note that there is no logical connection between realizing that a set of ground rules for public life are necessary and endorsing conservative politics.

Let us turn finally to the paradox of Proust's work already noted, that of his call for moral order in the face of an awareness of the variability of human experience. A negative consideration comes to mind immediately. Proust's novel is famous for its opening scene in which the young Marcel is able to get his way, so as to have his mother come and read in his room. The narrator of the novel returns to this scene time and time again, and ends up concluding that the father, who had opposed the exercise of the son's will, was irresponsible in the arbitrary way in which he gave in; his behavior is then contrasted with that of the mother and grandmother, even though their consistency at times causes them pain.[35] But their position is upheld and the father criticized. The novel suggests that absence of standards in his early life has made it all the harder for Marcel to develop the willpower that he needs to become an artist, someone able to arrest the confusion of life. The point at issue has been neatly summed

[33] Dahrendorf, *Society and Democracy in Germany*, 295.
[34] Riesman, *The Lonely Crowd*, part 3, "Autonomy."
[35] R. Shattuck, *Proust* (London: Fontana, 1974), 17.

up: "Not to know who you are is as bad as not knowing what you are."[36] In other words, a child needs something to react to if he or she is ever to be anything. Still more important is the need to note the functional nature of fronts and masks. On one occasion Goffman noted that "a disguise may function not so much as a way of concealing something as a way of revealing as much of it as can be tolerated in an encounter."[37] Masks are often, as Oscar Wilde had insisted, enabling in other ways. If one is unsure of a situation, then playing a role may be reassuring.[38] More important, it is through and behind masks that people have the freedom to find their identity. As Proust made clear, this freedom is all too often not pleasant. It is not a question of choosing roles, as some existentialist critics would have us believe, but of learning how to control and understand the roles we have been, and continue to be, forced to play.

With this in mind it becomes possible to explain why the politics of authenticity are bound to become authoritarian. The personal self has at its core the insistence that people do not have a real self, always available at the slightest touch of introspection. On the contrary, they can establish something like this, an identity able to integrate the intermittences of life, through time and effort, and with luck. Hence, any political theory that seeks to anchor human personality at one particular point and prevents people, for example, from making mistakes, and hopefully learning

---

[36] D. Martin, *Two Critiques of Spontaneity* (London: London School of Economics, 1974), 16.
[37] Goffman, "Role Distance," 69.
[38] Martin, *Two Critiques*, 25.

from them, is bound to end up coercing people into one particular mold.

This chapter has suggested that the social practices described by Goffman are those of civility; they deserve support in the face of critics who suggest that people should refuse to tarnish their real selves with such tawdry and inauthentic behavior. Given that "uniqueness" is supposedly desirable, the demand for greater authenticity in personal affairs seems forceful. The argument has been that this is not so. Once we realize that the practices described by Goffman are not sinister, then the demand to abolish them loses its emotional force, and can be evaluated calmly. Unrestricted openness and authenticity would lead to confusion, distrust, and, perhaps, the creation of ground rules of even more questionable character. Most important, the fronts and masks that are at the center of the social practices that Goffman describes are to be welcomed in allowing people to establish identities of their own, at their own pace. In contrast, the belief that we have a real self always available has been regarded as facile, and the consequent demand for authenticity as potentially dangerous. A final reason may be given for rating Goffman's work so highly. He is a skeptic. This is surely a merit in face of the great number of pseudofaiths on offer. One such pseudofaith that his work encourages us to distrust is the demand for authenticity.

CHAPTER 7

The Disenchantment of the Intellectuals

Many contemporary artists and intellectuals tell us that we are miserable. We have seen Rousseau's view of our psychic distress, caused by endlessly seeking to be something or someone else, imagining the grass to be greener on the other side of the fence, always wanting. Nietzsche added tremendous bite to such themes by lending a biological base to a moral critique. The influence of both can be seen in Sartre's insistence that there is a generalized problem of being. Equally, Heidegger claimed that we face a "void," particularly given our enslavement to high technology. We have more recently been told that we live in a world of risk in which "the life-world" is "colonized," and our humanity placed at a discount by the "malaise" of "modernity."[1] And such views are decidedly present in modern art, these days deeply influenced by social theory—prone indeed to quote such authors as Wittgenstein and Heidegger. One significant book about modern art notes the concentration on depression, seen as the pervasive mentality of "modernity."[2]

[1] U. Beck, *Risk Society: Towards a New Modernity* (London: Sage, 1992); J. Habermas, *The Theory of Communicative Action*, 2 vols. (Cambridge: Polity Press, 1984, 1987); C. Taylor, *The Malaise of Modernity* (Toronto: Anansi, 1991).

[2] C. Ross, *The Aesthetics of Disengagement: Contemporary Art and Depression* (Minneapolis: University of Minnesota Press, 2006).

The most evocative label capturing such discontent is disenchantment, and its subtlest exponent Max Weber. His work centers around the "rationalization of the world," but only a single lecture, "Science as a Vocation," directly considers the consequences of this process for the way in which we feel, or, more precisely, for our social identity. Science does not, Weber argued, make modern man better informed than the Hottentot; instead it means

> the knowledge or belief that if one but wished one *could* learn at any time. Hence, it means that principally there are no mysterious incalculable forces that come into play, but rather that one can, in principle, master all things by calculation. This means that the world is disenchanted.[3]

Weber is describing the opportunity/cost of modernity: science brings plenty, but it destroys warm and comfortable identities. This claim haunts much of modern social theory. Weber himself was ambivalent, scornful of cheap "re-enchanting" creeds but not above hoping that charisma might provide us with passionate attachment to some new cause. Weber's agenda can be clearly seen more recently in the title of the lecture that the German philosopher Jürgen Habermas gave when receiving the Hegel Prize in 1974. "Can modern societies build a rational identity?" he asked, before replying firmly in the positive.

A Pandora's box of claims and implications, descriptive

---

[3] M. Weber, "Science as a Vocation" (1919), in *From Max Weber: Essays in Sociology*, ed. H. H. Gerth and C. W. Mills ([1948] New York: Oxford University Press, 1970), 139.

and normative, must be opened to cast light on these issues. Should we believe this strand of modern culture? Given what has been said, the answer will be negative. Is it then the case that our cherished belief in art, as illuminating our condition, should be abandoned? It is useful here to recall immediately a Durkheimian principle: every sign has a social referent and this, when interpreted, will tell us something about reality. The argument will add to what has been said to this point by showing that the set of ideas in question tells us more about the social position of some intellectuals than about our general social condition. When such figures seek to remold others so as to manage their own needs, they are likely to become enemies of civility. But it is very important here to make distinctions, both about art in general and about the scope of conditions under which intellectuals can be dangerous. We can advance understanding by considering the sociologies of culture of Daniel Bell and Pierre Bourdieu, interestingly and amusingly at odds with each other. As there are complexities to the argument, it may be good to clarify one point in advance: it is not the case that all intellectuals are enemies of civility, though some certainly are, with the impact of intellectuals depending less on ideas than on structural conditions.

But let us begin with the general claim about our putative misery. There is everything to be said for skepticism. Poverty, disease, and early mortality—that is, the standard condition of preindustrial life—were scarcely enchanting. There is, of course, little direct evidence about the feelings of the vast majority of humankind until relatively recently in the historical record. But we have some—such as the account of life in the Pyrenees in the early fourteenth century—and it brings home the suffering inherent to this condition.[4] Perhaps the modern world is bereft of meaning, but the affluence provided by modern science means that for the vast majority of people, the world has probably never been so enchanted. The romantic nostalgia so characteristic of modernist ideas is unlikely to have any general appeal once industrial conditions have been established. Curiously, there is very little empirical investigation into the purported misery of modern men and women, and certainly few findings to back up the view that disenchantment dominates most of social life. In contrast, there is a massive amount of evidence supporting Adam Smith's view of people being distracted from questions of meaning by the demands of status competition. And we should not forget the positive side of such competition, the benefits of fashion, of trying on new selves, of self-expression.

This leads to the central point: artists and intellectuals have their own particular worries, and so may not give an accurate report on modern social conditions. In premodern, status-dominated societies, the prestige of intellectuals was often huge, not least given that literacy was not widespread but rather their preserve. The decline in standing has been very great. Nineteenth-century Russian thinkers wrote more eloquently than any others about this situation, in large part because of the schizophrenia induced by knowledge of the developed West while living in a backward society. Mikhail Petrashevsky exemplified this world of "superfluous men" when he decided to devote himself to the service of mankind after realizing that he had no particular links to or ad-

---

[4] E. Le Roy Ladurie, *Montaillou: The Promised Land of Error* (New York: G. Braziller, 1978).

miration for the men and women of his own social circle. He became a follower of the French socialist Charles Fourier, and so established a commune on his estate: the peasants hated it and burned it down. Petrashevsky was close to Fyodor Dostoyevsky, whose great novel *The Devils* famously captured the tensions within this world. Of course, patronage at times replaced the status that came with the monopoly of literacy, but patrons can be and indeed were often fickle. So intellectuals and artists had to exist in the interstices of the market. Naturally enough, they sometimes felt badly done by, with their works accurately reflecting this experience, as Henry David Thoreau noted:

I believe that what so saddens the reformer is not his sympathy with his fellows in distress but, though he be the holiest son of God, is his private ail. Let this be righted, let the spring come to him, the morning rise over his couch, and he will forsake his generous companions without apology.[5]

This baseline condition could be exacerbated by the overproduction and so underemployment of the educated. Thomas Hobbes felt that this contributed to the English civil war, and there seems evidence that this was so—certainly thereafter attempts were made by the elite to limit the production of the educated.[6] Joseph Schumpeter particu-

[5] H. D. Thoreau, *Walden, or, Life in the Woods*, ed. L. Ross ([1854] New York: Sterling, 2009), 98–99.
[6] T. Hobbes, *Behemoth, or the Long Parliament* ([1681] Chicago: University of Chicago Press, 1990). The empirical evidence is that of M. Curtis, "The

larly stressed in this regard that capitalism tended to over-produce intellectuals:

> All those who are unemployed or unsatisfactorily employed or unemployable drift into the vocations in which standards are least definite or in which aptitudes and acquirements of a different order count. They swell the host of intellectuals in the strict sense of the term whose numbers hence increase disproportionately. They enter it in a thoroughly discontented frame of mind. Discontent breeds resentment. And it often rationalizes itself into that social criticism which as we have seen before is in any case the intellectual spectator's typical attitude toward men, classes and institutions especially in a rationalist and utilitarian civilization. Well, here we have numbers; a well-defined group situation of proletarian hue; and a group interest shaping a group attitude that will much more realistically account for hostility to the capitalist order than could the theory—itself a rationalization in the psychological sense—according to which the intellectual's righteous indignation about the wrongs of capitalism simply represents the logical inference from outrageous facts and which is no better than the theory of lovers that their feelings represent nothing but the logical inference from the virtues of the beloved.[7]

Alienated Intellectuals of Early Stuart England," *Past and Present*, no. 23 (1962).

[7] J. Schumpeter, *Capitalism, Socialism and Democracy* ([1942] London: Routledge, 1978), 153.

Schumpeter, however, did not believe that the intellectuals could *themselves* overturn capitalism. Rather, he suggested that they would highlight and accentuate resentments that other groups already had against capitalism. "Labour never craved intellectual leadership," he noted, "but intellectuals invaded labour politics."[8] An interesting variation on this theme is Tocqueville's view that intellectuals will differ: the great dreamers of authoritarian schemes are those who lack social engagement, whereas those who have access to power—Adam Smith and Maynard Keynes jump immediately to the forefront of attention—will feel less isolated, and so produce theories in which their own needs are not hegemonic. And it is impossible not to quote Samuel Johnson, who was aware that intellectuals can suffer from the dangers of imagination at all times:

> To indulge the power of fiction, and send imagination out upon the wing, is often the sport of those who delight too much in silent speculation. When we are alone we are not always busy; the labour of excogitation is too violent to last long; the ardour of enquiry will sometimes give way to idleness or satiety. He who has nothing external that can divert him, must find pleasure in his own thoughts, and must conceive himself what he is not; for who is pleased with what he is? He then expatiates in boundless futurity, and culls from all imaginable conditions that which for the present moment he should most desire, amuses his desires with impossible enjoyments, and confers upon

[8] Ibid.

his pride unattainable dominion. The mind dances from scene to scene, unites all pleasures in all combinations, and riots in delights which nature and fortune, with all their bounty, cannot bestow.[9]

This is the moment to begin to make distinctions, and we can do so in the spirit of Tocqueville's awareness of differences in the behavior of intellectuals. Let us begin by considering the claim that art is by inherent necessity and logic humanist and liberal, with those who endorse horrible practices thereby being seen as mere ideologists lacking all aesthetic virtue. This cannot be wholly true. Whatever one may think of Heidegger, it is hard to deny that Louis-Ferdinand Céline is a great writer, and D. W. Griffith a superb director—and both made illiberal sentiments comprehensible, even attractive. There have been intellectual justifications for racism, murder, and every sort of foulness, often embraced with enthusiasm. Still, there is something to the claim. An awareness of the absurdity of life, its lack of meaning, is surely in a fundamental way totally correct. No one understood this more and wrote about it better than Samuel Beckett. The absurdity he portrayed was, of course, so deep that all one could do was to live with it, no escape being possible. Interestingly, his work is full of humor and irony, his life marked by considerable courage. The trouble comes with those who cannot stand emptiness, and who believe that it is possible and necessary to escape it. It was not a long step for Joseph Goebbels to move from his early ex-

[9] S. Johnson, *Rasselas, Prince of Abyssinia*, in *Rasselas, Poems and Selected Prose*, ed. B. H. Bronson ([1759] New York: Holt, Rinehart & Winston, 1966), 596.

pressionist novel to the embrace of a new creed. This again is the world of belonging and authenticity. One is reminded at this point of the comment made by Raymond Aron to his teacher Léon Brunschvicg when he returned from Nazi Germany in the early 1930s—namely, that the Nuremburg Rallies were pure Durkheim, "society worshipping itself." To turn complex society into a singular, moral community in modern times has always required force. It is better to live with less.

How worried should we be about this tendency in modern culture? A helpful way to approach these issues is by looking at the two sociologists who offer interesting ideas about the effect of art on society, beginning with Daniel Bell, who suggested nothing less than that capitalism is facing its demise as a result of a cultural contradiction.[10] His argument is that capitalism was able to work as a political, economic, and cultural system only as a result of the presence of religion. He does not clearly spell out the benefits of religion (although he waxes eloquent on the evil consequences of their loss) but some of his hints in the matter are worth noting. Puritanism is important in that its values serve to bind together all three realms mentioned. The puritan ethic is of obvious economic value. Bell hints that it is also of political value in encouraging people to make their own fates independently of the state; for many years this underwrote the pluralism of American politics that was responsible for diffusing social conflict. But most important in Bell's eyes is that puritanism offers some answers in the

---

[10] A very similar claim, albeit in a different register, is made by Jürgen Habermas in *Legitimation Crisis* (London: Heinemann, 1976).

cultural realm. Bell's conception of culture stresses that it is a response to the basic questions of the human predicament, most notably that of death. The answers provided by religion gave meaning to life, and the presence of such meaning gave a guarantee of social stability.

This unity has now collapsed so that the polity, economy, and culture run on different "axial principles." The economy is concerned with ever-increasing economic growth but is disrupted by excessive wage demands that cause inflation. The polity is concerned with establishing legitimacy but is troubled by insistent demands for political participation. Bell is not, in the last analysis, worried by these problems for which he sees relatively easy solutions, but he is terrified by modern culture, which he feels is now based on a remorseless demand for the fulfillment of rampant individualism. Bell's fears can only be understood when one realizes that his Jewish background placed the Holocaust at the center of his social theory. Bell believes that human beings, bereft of the restraint imposed by a religious order, are likely to seek salvation through domination. The demonic is released when there is no longer assurance that life has meaning:

> Religion ... was a way for people to cope with the problem of death. . . . When it was possible to believe, really believe, in heaven and hell, then some of the fear of death could be tempered or controlled. . . .
>
> It may well be that the decline in religious *faith* in the last century and more, this fear of death as total annihilation, unconsciously expressed, has probably increased. One may hypothesise, in fact, that here is a

cause of the breakthrough of the irrational, which is
such a marked feature of the changed moral temper of
our time. Fanaticism, violence, and cruelty are not, of
course, unique in human history. But there was a time
when such frenzies and mass emotions could be displaced, symbolised, drained away, and dispersed
through religious devotion and practice. Now there is
only this life, and the assertion of self becomes possible—for some even necessary—in the domination
over others.[11]

Bell's fears, then, are not just for the breakdown of social
structure but rather for the reemergence of the demonic. Art
was placed under restraint in religious cultures, but it has
now, in Bell's eyes, achieved autonomy; in other words, the
investigation into the meaning of life has recently been undertaken by art. The autonomy of art is seen in and is responsible for modernism, that cultural mode that Bell feels
reached its peak in the years 1890–1920. Modernism represents one of the greatest moments of human creativity in his
eyes, and allows the aesthetic imagination to lay bare the im-
pulses of the human mind. He considers modernism's central figures to be Dostoyevsky and Nietzsche, both of whom
glorified those roots of impulse concerned with sexuality
and will to power.

Bell's fears for the social stability of modern capitalism
depend on his going beyond this thesis on modernism to
stress the danger of "modernism in the streets." The great

---

[11] D. Bell, *The End of Ideology: On the Exhaustion of Political Ideas in the Fifties*,
2nd rev. ed. (New York: Free Press, 1962), 400–401.

classics had at least obeyed the restraints of artistic form. Bell's hatred of many contemporary cultural phenomena follows from his belief that all restraints have vanished. The facile and meretricious popularizations of modernism scare him:

> When there is the democratization of Dionysius in the acting out of one's impulses, then the demonic spills over all bounds, and suffers a double fate. At one extreme, violence becomes the aesthetic of politics (no longer of art), as in the calls to a cleansing of the polluted selves by a Sorel, a Marinetti, a Sartre, or a Fanon; at the other, the demonic becomes trivialised in the masochistic exorcisms of the cultural mass.[12]

By the latter point, Bell seems to mean that, to use his expression, "pornotopia" sets the tone for popular culture; and this—despite his comment about "trivialisation"—is a source of worry in that Bell feels that something once thought can later serve as the basis for action.

One central ambiguity in Bell's account should be highlighted. He wishes to scare and to reassure, and this makes for a most contradictory analysis. The social reformer holds out the hope that

> despite the shambles of modern culture, some religious answer surely will be forthcoming, for religion is not (or no longer) a "property" of society in the Durk-

---

[12] D. Bell, "The Return of the Sacred? The Argument on the Future of Religion," *British Journal of Sociology* 28 (1977): 431.

heimian sense. It is a constitutive part of man's consciousness: the cognitive search for the pattern of the
"general order" of existence; the affective need to establish rituals and to make such conceptions sacred;
the primordial need for relatedness to some others, or
to a set of meanings which will establish a transcen-
dent response of the self; and the existential need to
confront the finalities of suffering and death.[13]

This is vague, and open to the classic objection that understanding the function of religion is not the same as understanding the religious impulse itself. People do not believe
because it is good for them but because there is a theology
that helps them make sense of the world. Further, there is
something unbalanced about Bell's account of the unre-
leased human demon and his hope for a new religion. If
what modernism has released is demonic, then surely its very
power as psychic dynamite prevents it being easily curtailed.
Bell himself seems to consider this a possibility:

But the postmodern mood, touching deeper springs of
human consciousness, and deeper, more restless long-
ings than the overt political search for community, is
only the first act of a drama that is still to be played
out.[14]

[13] D. Bell, *The Cultural Contradictions of Capitalism* (London: Heinemann,
1976), 169.
[14] D. Bell, *The Winding Passage: Sociological Essays and Journeys* (New Bruns-
wick, NJ: Transaction, 300.

Bell oscillates between his hopes and the conclusions to which his analysis seems to be forcing him.

One of the amusing characteristics of social studies—making one reluctant to talk too easily of social *science*—is the fame and attention given to wholly opposing theories. The second analysis of the effects of modern art is derived from Western Marxism. Thinkers in this school are naturally much exercised by the failure of Marx's prediction that revolution would usher in a new order. Not surprisingly, many have suggested that various factors in the "superstructure" are restraining the natural outcome of objective factors. This line of investigation has spiritual ancestors in the work of Lukács, Gramsci, and the Frankfurt School, perhaps especially in that of Herbert Marcuse. However, attention is worth giving to those writers of the French Left who have given added sophistication to this approach by concentrating on art. And by art they are concerned not with the popular trash of "the culture industry" but with supposedly high and meritorious art. Their general theory is simple. The bourgeoisie is deemed to pose as the protectors of culture, and this is held to be sociologically crucial in justifying their class advantage. Thus schematized, the position sounds most implausible; this makes it all the more to the credit of Pierre Bourdieu (*marxisant* rather than Marxist) and Renée Balibar that they are able to give it some plausibility as the result of empirical work. The general theory as to the function and political consequences of art may be described best by looking at Bourdieu's work; the question of quality becomes more clearly focused when turning to Balibar.

Bourdicu's work on the sociology of art is part of a much larger project concerned with arguing that bourgeois society exerts "symbolic violence" in establishing a "cultural arbitrary" that is not justified by philosophic reasoning. However, all that we need to realize here is that he considers that art is a key means by which the bourgeoisie makes its own rule seem natural. Bourdieu feels that this can clearly be seen in the process of art perception itself. He notes that it is in fact difficult to "read" the pictures of previous civilizations: one needs, for example, considerable knowledge of the iconography of the Renaissance to understand Florentine fifteenth-century painting. Bourdieu then suggests that:

> Since the work of art only exists to the extent that it is perceived, or in other words deciphered, it goes without saying that the satisfactions attached to this perception . . . are only accessible to those who are disposed to appropriate them because they *attribute a value to them*, it being understood that they can do this only if they have the means to appropriate them.[15]

The training and educational standards necessary to decipher works of art would lead one to expect that the difficulty of understanding would be generally acknowledged. Bourdieu feels that the opposite is the case; this horrifies him. He considers that the most connoisseured are keenest

---

[15] P. Bourdieu, "Outlines of a Sociological Theory of Art Perception," *International Social Science Journal* 20 (1968): 601. Cf. P. Bourdieu, *Distinction: A Sociological Critique of the Judgement of Taste* (Cambridge, MA: Harvard University Press, 1984).

to stress that art is the product of inexplicable genius, and that it is capable of moving anyone with sensitivity. He acidly comments that

> silence concerning the social prerequisites for the appropriation of culture or, to be more exact, for the acquisition of art competence in the sense of mastery of all the means for the specific appropriation of works of art is a self-seeking silence because it is what makes it possible to legitimatize a social privilege by pretending that it is a gift of nature.[16]

The bourgeoisie thus poses as the agent of civilization and justifies its position on this ground, while making it difficult for the mass of the population to understand the mysteries of culture that it apparently guards. Bourdieu feels that he has found evidence for this argument in an empirical study of the image of museums in various European countries. He is able to show without much difficulty that museums are used by the highly educated, who may be described as possessors of an "extended code" of culture; in contrast, the mass of the population, possessors of a more "restricted code" of culture, are afraid of museums and tend to associate them with churches.[17] And Bourdieu is once again keen to argue that this fear is not surprising given that so little attempt is made to help ignorant viewers once they are actually inside a museum.

Bourdieu's position is one that is best seen as moderate in

[16] Bourdieu, "Outlines of a Sociological Theory," 608.
[17] P. Bourdieu and A. Darbel, L'Amour de L'Art (Paris: Minuet, 1969).

that it seems to suggest that great art should be made available to more than the few. This stance naturally leads to calls
for reform and may be contrasted with more radical versions
of the social control theory of art. These extreme versions
argue for the abolition of bourgeois art on the basis of the
sociological premise: the discovery that art is the preserve of
the few quickly leads to the assertion that it cannot be of
high quality. These extreme versions often have as a starting
point the observation that turning art into a barrier of social
distinction militates against artistic appreciation. In particular, it is claimed that art can only serve as a barrier to the
understanding of normal people if taste is made to change
quickly. The increased speed with which taste changes in
modern society is neatly captured by a wholly different figure, Quentin Bell:

> Novelty, audacity, and above all exclusiveness, the
> bright badge of social enterprise brings a fashion in,
> and when a hat or shoe has lost its social appeal, when
> everybody is wearing it, it dies of popularity. Such
> seems to be the fate of elitist art in our society, the so-
> cial impulse that made it fashionable with the few
> ends by making it vulgar with the many whereupon
> the elite must look for something else.[18]

Such sentiments serve as a starting point for Balibar's recent work in the sociology of literature. She argues that the
French educational system manages to buttress the position

[18] Q. Bell, *A Demotic Art* (Southampton: University of Southampton, 1976), 8.

of the bourgeoisie in many ways. The very national language that was established in the revolutionary period was based on the grammars of the Old Regime that centered on the need to translate French into Latin; this allowed different "levels" of French to develop thereafter.[19] Literature plays a central role in developing these levels of language in three ways. First, authors themselves were deeply affected by the new emphasis on style. George Sand, for example, spent much of her time in the early 1840s collecting examples of local speech, but none of this was included in the fictional treatment she gave of the same rural workers in *La Mare au Diable*.[20] Much the same is true of Flaubert. Balibar spends a great deal of time analyzing the styles of speech of the characters in *A Simple Heart* and interestingly notes that all, and especially the servant Félicité, speak perfect French. Balibar is not one to shirk sweeping conclusions and concludes in this instance that the bourgeoisie was attempting to make the lower orders mute. Second, she considers that examination of the manner in which literature came to be taught in French schools justifies speaking of different levels of cultural comprehension; in the primary school, literary passages are used for dictation and comprehension only, whereas in the secondary school the pupil is introduced to the author's work as a whole and trained in an appreciation of the value of literary creativity. This latter emphasis is deemed particularly unfortunate in that it results in a "sacralizing" of the text that removes it from the comprehension that can only be gained by placing it in its social con-

[19] R. Balibar and D. Laporte, *Le Francais National* (Paris: Hachette, 1974).
[20] R. Balibar, *Les Francais Fictifs* (Paris: Hachette, 1976), 42.

text. This forms the basis of her third point, made as the result of empirical work on the schoolbooks of French children. She argues that books that do have radical intent (Zola's novels dealing with alcoholism is an example cited) tend to be "misread" when they are used as school texts; the emphasis on style apparently obscures the obvious political message.[21]

Balibar's claim is that bourgeois mentality is hostile to real culture. John Berger's celebrated claim that many classic genres of bourgeois art—portrait, landscape, and nude— are meretricious, the glorification of position and property, is similar. Art too closely reflects its social origin; and in this case art suffers from the original sin of being the child of the bourgeoisie. Berger carries on his argument by suggesting that the abolition of the art of the few will help raise artistic standards. He sees "no reason to lament the passing of the portrait—the talent once involved in portrait painting can be used in some other way to serve a more urgent, modern function."[22] It is not surprising to find this position argued by a Marxist, although it does go against Marx's insistence that the new society would accommodate the cultural achievements of the bourgeoisie.

The most obvious weakness that springs to mind as we begin to evaluate these views is the implicit assumption that the values of modernist "high art" have come to dominate the tone of the general culture. Evidence in the sociology of literature on this matter goes in the opposite direction. Romantic novels and popular drama remain remarkably con-

[22] J. Berger, *The Look of Things* (London: Viking Press, 1972), 35.

servative in their moral emphasis.[23] Bell's analysis is here amusingly at odds with that of the Frankfurt School, which accurately noted the conservative character of much popular art, and condemned it precisely for this "ascetic" character. Bell has little sense of where his allies lie; he would perhaps do better to join with those who use the "common sense" of popular art as a tool with which to berate the pretensions of high culture. And this finding does nearly as much to undermine the view that access to culture serves as a mechanism enabling the privileged to pass on their advantages. As a Marxist theory this is, of course, weird: it seems as if brute material forces are constrained by the upper reaches of the superstructure! This is idealism with a vengeance, and it conjures up amusing thoughts of the leaders of the revolution marching under banners calling for the death of "bourgeois high culture." Perhaps there is something to the view insofar as it is part of the competitive emulation described by Adam Smith, especially as it applies to higher levels of the class structure. But there is no real evidence that the disadvantaged are somehow mystified by the presence of cultural matters that they do not understand. British experience certainly suggests that this is mistaken.[24]

It is also important to note that Bell's account of modernism is exaggerated. Samuel Beckett does not fit within his account, nor do *Ulysses* and *À la recherche du temps perdu.*

[23] J.S.R. Goodlad, *A Sociology of Popular Drama* (London: Heinemann, 1972); P. Mann, *Books, Borrowers and Buyers* (London: Andre Deutsch, 1969).
[24] R. Bourne, "The Snakes and Ladders of the British Class System," in *New Society* 47 (1979): 242. Much more evidence supporting this position can be found in A. H. Halsey, A. F. Heath, and J. M. Ridge, *Origins and Destinations* (Oxford: Oxford University Press, 1980).

Molly Bloom's soliloquy in the former is popularly and justly known as nothing less than one of the great affirmations of "life itself." In the latter Marcel, after much strain and anguish at the "intermittences of the heart," establishes an identity for himself: the last volume of the book, *Time Regained*, is a paean of praise for the value of his newly found artistic vocation. Then Proust's awareness of human instability leads him to argue forcefully for the preservation of moral standards—and he insists time and again that his moments of involuntary memory are useless to him without the disciplined determination to investigate their meaning fully.[25] And in this Proust is in fact representative of modernism in general, which is best seen not as an attack on reason but as an attempt to understand the full workings of the human heart. Freud's work is based on the discovery that seemingly irrational behavior is in fact perfectly rational.

But let us put those considerations aside, as we must, given that there is without any question a major strand of modern culture that does make much of our disenchanted status, very often proposing in consequence to find ways in which to re-enchant us. Many have noticed and analyzed the enormous ideological pool of re-enchantment so often formed from fusions of Marx and Freud, but not every analyst has thereby judged capitalism to be under threat.

> A really advanced industrial society does not any longer require cold rationality from its consumers; at most, it may demand it of its producers. But as it gets more advanced, the ratio both of personnel and of

[25] M. Hindus, *The Proustian Vision*, especially the chapter "Ethics."

their time is tilted progressively more and more in favour of consumption, as against production. More consumers, fewer producers: less time at work, more at leisure. And in consumption, all tends towards ease and facility of manipulation rather than rigour and coldness. A modern piece of machinery may be a marvel of sustained, abstract, rigorous engineering thought; but its operating controls must be such that they can easily and rapidly be internalised by the average user, without arduousness or strain. So the user lives in a world in which most things have an air of easy, "natural," "spontaneous" manipulability. And why should not the world itself be conceived in this manner?[26]

Interestingly, Bell makes essentially the same point:

Today one finds asceticism primarily in revolutionary movements and revolutionary regimes. Puritanism, in the psychological and sociological sense, is to be found in Communist China and in the regimes which fuse revolutionary sentiment with Koranic purposes, as in Algeria and Libya.[27]

Revolutions are indeed made or led by intolerant elites; it is hard to see the antinomian, sex-ridden, and self-indulgent popularizers of modernism as being capable of destroying anything. Settled conditions in the industrial era place intel-

[26] E. A. Gellner, "Ethnomethodology: The Re-enchantment Industry or The Californian Way of Subjectivity," *Philosophy of Social Sciences* 5 (1975): 448.
[27] Bell, *The Cultural Contradictions*, 82.

lectuals at a discount; their demands for re-enchantment
amount to mere cultural entertainment. At present this is
the world of Slavoj Žižek and Alain Badiou, who are amaz-
ingly blind to the past, mere apologists for horror. But it be-
hooves us to remain aware of the fact that times are not always settled. Great social transitions and the disruptions
caused by defeat in war can create social conditions in which
intellectuals gain great influence. So we should remain wary
of the gifts offered by intellectuals.

In conclusion, let us return to Max Weber. In purely philosophical terms, some of his arguments are impossible to
ignore. The cognitive power of science is immense, and it
does put traditional belief at a discount. Our acceptance of
empiricism, the base of real knowledge, means that facts
stand over us, beyond our control. In that sense we are and
must be disenchanted. But the tenor in which Weber writes
about this is far too Germanic, far too close to the cultural
pessimism so prevalent in the society in which he lived. The
suggestion is that life is cold and without meaning because
we have become homunculi, workers, so to speak, in factories whose production depends on the dull rigidities of
assembly lines. But the point about assembly lines, to continue the metaphor, is that they produce endless technological marvels that anyone can use, and that increase choice
and expand horizons. And there is a related point that needs
to be made about Weber. His scorn for sloppy, facile, re-
enchanting creeds is admirable. Habermas's call for a rich,
rational social identity can be seen in this regard as wholly
question-begging. But Weber was not above seeking to
warm up the world when insisting that charismatic renewal

CHAPTER 8

The Problem with Communism

There is a curiosity about communism. Normally, there is much to be said for Kierkegaard's view that we live our life forward and understand it backward. This applies in many ways to communism, now that it has all but gone. But some of the intellectual tools hinting at why it was likely to fail were present before the communist regimes of the modern world were instituted at the end of the First World War. This, seen in the light of sociological theory and the historical record, is the initial concern of this chapter. The second half of the chapter uses the insight gained to comment on the character of communism and on the nature of its demise.

It is good to begin with Karl Marx's utopian vision, so clearly influenced by romanticism, and, above all, by the view that human beings should be complete and unitary, that is, free from any sort of psychic splitting.[1] This is made especially clear in his famous characterization of communist society:

---

[1] L. Kolakowski, "The Myth of Human Self-Identity: Unity of Civil and Political Society in Socialist Thought," in *The Socialist Idea: A Reappraisal*, ed. L. Kolakowski and S. Hampshire (London: Weidenfeld and Nicolson, 1974).

was needed to release us from the dull slough of mere materialism. In this matter, Weber seems to me to be not nearly disenchanted enough. Life really does not have a meaning, as Smith realized when speaking of "winter storms," and as Beckett stresses all the time. To pretend otherwise is infantile. The warm and cozy worlds of the re-enchanters are deeply unconvincing, an extra reason—beyond its link to science—why openness is positively morally attractive. Anomie is better than bonhomie!

As soon as the distribution of labour comes into being, each man has a particular, exclusive sphere of activity, which is forced upon him and from which he cannot escape. He is a hunter, a fisherman, a shepherd, or a critical critic, and must remain so if he does not want to lose his means of livelihood; while in communist society, where nobody has one exclusive sphere of activity but each can become accomplished in any branch he wishes, society regulates the general production and thus makes it possible for me to do one thing today and another tomorrow, to hunt in the morning, fish in the afternoon, rear cattle in the evening, criticize after dinner, just as I have a mind, without ever becoming hunter, fisherman, shepherd or critic.[2]

It was once believed that this early romantic humanism was left behind, replaced later by "scientific" socialism. But these early attitudes remain implicit in the later thought. Why should we jump on the historical bandwagon; that is, why should we accept, rather than seek to delay, the various historical stages identified by the materialist conception of history? The answer to this question is surely that the earlier thought reveals an essential human nature that existed before class society, thereby assuring us that the process of history is creating something that is not just inevitable but also both practical and desirable.

[2] K. Marx and F. Engels, *The German Ideology*, in *The Marx-Engels Reader*, ed. R. W. Tucker ([1846] New York: W. W. Norton, 1960), 160.

Émile Durkheim wished to differentiate himself from Marx, so he gave lectures on early socialism that can be seen as an attempt to draw his students away from a false trail and toward the proper one: sociology. Everything in his view depends on the distinction drawn between communism and socialism:

> One school labels as antisocial everything which is private property, in a general way, while the other considers dangerous only the individual appropriation of the large economic enterprises which are established at a specific moment in history. Therefore, their significant motives are not at all the same. Communism is prompted by moral and timeless reasons; socialism by considerations of an economic sort. For the former, private property must be abolished because it is the source of all immorality; for the latter, the vast industrial and commercial enterprises cannot be left to themselves, as they affect too profoundly the entire economic life of society. Their conclusions are so different because one sees the remedy only in a suppression, as complete as possible, of economic interests; the other, in their socialization.[3]

Durkheim suggests that the social carriers of communism are dreamers, isolated intellectuals unrepresentative of any broader social current. In contrast, he takes socialism much more seriously: it may well be that socialist ideas are pro-

---

[3] E. Durkheim, *Socialism*, trans. C. Sattler ([1928] New York: Macmillan, 1962), 75.

duced by intellectuals, but their appeal is wide because the working class—the carriers of Marx's vision—are not properly integrated into modern society. Nonetheless, Durkheim insists that socialism does not answer to their suffering because it stands far too close to the world that it seeks to replace. In particular, it seeks merely to spread material goods around, and so fails to regulate appetites. This is a recipe for disaster:

> It is a general law of all living things that needs and appetites are normal only on condition of being controlled. Unlimited need contradicts itself. For need is defined by the goal it aims at, and if unlimited has no goal—since there is no limit. It is no true aim, to seek constantly more than one has—to work in order to overtake the point one has reached, with a view only to exceeding that point . . . an appetite that nothing can appease can never be satisfied. Insatiable thirst can only be a source of suffering. Whatever one does, it is never slaked. . . . In its normal state sexual desire is aroused for a time, then is appeased. With the erotomaniac there are no limits.[4]

As is so often the case, Marx and Durkheim have much in common, seeing social processes as being in large part derived from the bottom up. With Max Weber we enter an entirely different world, as can be seen first in negative and then in positive terms.

---

[4] Ibid., 239–40.

Weber did not feel that there was an inevitable link between the working class and socialism. Insofar as the working class had embraced socialist ideals, and this was by no means totally so, this was due, as noted in chapter 3, to the antisocialist policies of the state. Such policies prevented demands being made at the industrial level, thereby making it necessary for workers to "take on" the state. He makes similar points about the peasantry, especially outside the Occident.[5] He follows Durkheim in arguing that modern communism seeks to manage the economy rather than to abolish it. But he insists against Durkheim that communism is "indifferent to calculation" and hence oblivious to any "consideration of means for obtaining an optimum of provisions"; what matters instead are "direct feelings of mutual solidarity."[6]

Further, Weber's positive analysis has a different spirit from that of his French contemporary. In particular, he specifies three social bases for premodern communism. Household communism is, so to speak, natural, and he held it to exist in some large financial houses even in his own day.[7] This form of communism has no trace of any communistic practices concerning women, and it does not provide any sort of model for the larger society.[8] This is not true of military communism, analyzed in the middle of a long section dealing with charisma:

[5] M. Weber, *Economy and Society*, ed. and trans. G. Roth and C. Wittich ([1922] Berkeley: University of California Press, 1978), 469–70.
[6] Ibid., 42.
[7] Ibid., 300.
[8] Ibid., 363–64.

The communist warrior is the perfect counterpart to the monk, whose garrisoned and communistic life in the monastery serves the purpose of disciplining him in the service of his other-worldly master (and, resulting therefrom, perhaps also his this-worldly master). With consistent development of the warriors' community, the dissociation from the family and all private economic interests is found also outside the celibate knightly orders which were created in direct analogy to the monastic orders. The inmates of the men's house purchase or capture girls, or they claim that the girls of the subject community be at their disposal as long as they have not been sold in marriage. The children of the Areoi—the dominant status group in Polynesia—are killed. Men can join enduring sexual unions with a separate economy only after completing their service in the men's house—often only at an advanced age. The communist military organization, which is widely spread under conditions of chronic warfare and which requires warriors without home and family, may be reflected residually in several phenomena: differentiation according to age groups, which is sometimes also important for the regulation of sexual relationships; survivals of an allegedly primitive "endogamous promiscuity" or of a "primeval right" of all male warriors to all unappropriated women; likewise, abduction as the allegedly earliest forms of marriage, and above all the "matrilineal family."[9]

[9] Ibid., 1153.

But it is the third type that really matters. This is the sharing inside a charismatically bound religious group. Such sharing seems to be accepted because it is a temporary necessity. This leads Weber to a characteristic judgment when writing about early Christianity:

> Work attained dignity much later, beginning with the monastic orders who used it as an ascetic means. During the charismatic period of a religion, the perfect disciple must also reject landed property, and the mass of believers is expected to be indifferent towards it. An expression of this indifference is that attenuated form of the charismatic communism of love which apparently existed in the early Christian community of Jerusalem, where the members of the community owned property "as if they did not own it." Such unlimited, unrationalized sharing with needy brothers, which forced the missionaries, especially Paulus, to collect alms abroad for the anti-economic central community, is probably what lies behind that much-discussed tradition, not any allegedly "socialist" organization or communist "collective ownership." Once the eschatological expectations fade, charismatic communism in all its forms declines and retreats into monastic circles, where it becomes the special concern of the exemplary followers of God.[10]

That egalitarian sharing was encoded in one of the key documents of the Western tradition, the Acts of the Apostles,

[10] Ibid., 1187.

matters greatly from a Weberian point of view: it provided a moral legacy available to later European radicals. Nonetheless, if Marx was but the last of a long line of intellectuals to make use of that legacy, Weber's case remains that the generalized appeal of socialism in the modern world derives, as noted, from Old Regime politics—rather than being, as both Marx and Durkheim believe, an expression of society.

We can evaluate these theoretical claims by turning to the historical record with a definition in mind. Communism should be defined, first of all, as an attempt to institutionalize the sharing of land or women in the face of the complexity represented by agroliterate polities.[11] Consequently, communism is neither equality nor communalism: it is a dream of moral unity, an example of what Freud called "the oceanic feeling," in the face of complexities that are felt to be threatening. To stress all this is to disagree with Durkheim. This is particularly true of the distinction drawn between socialism and communism—a contrast that parallels that drawn by Élie Halévy between freedom and organization.[12] Certainly, some socialists—notably Sidney and Beatrice Webb—were keener on the extirpation of waste than on freedom; and it is quite correct to say that modern socialism does habitually take the problem of organizing the industrial machine very seriously. Nonetheless, modern socialism in the end is an example of communism: differently put, socialism is inconceivable without the emphasis on solidarity,

---

[11] This definition is that of Patricia Crone, with whom I once organized a conference on premodern communism.

[12] É. Halévy, "The Policy of Social Peace in England" and "The Problem of Worker Control," in his *The Era of Tyrannies: Essays on Socialism and War* ([1938] New York: Penguin, 1967).

equality, and sharing. In practice, socialism proved, of course, to be a hugely Durkheimian affair: the Webbs, for instance, were driven by moral purpose far more than by a penchant for economic planning. The purpose of socialism was that of creating a new moral order. In other words, the very nature of Marx's writings—the desire to abolish splitting *and* to have the benefits of advanced technology—makes nonsense of Durkheim's basic distinction.

The historical record shows that there were in fact three types of communism in premodern circumstance, each of which deserves brief discussion before general analytic points are made. The Greek world remembered a simpler tribal past for all that it possessed private—or at least house-hold—property. Perhaps this helps to explain—as does the endless constitutional thought consequent on experiments in colonization—why so many accounts of the communist practices of simpler peoples were produced.[13] It may well be that those simpler peoples were not communist at all, as is often the case with societies to whom communism is im-puted. Nonetheless, the texts themselves are evidence of ad-miration, even of longing for communist practices. Such dreams would have mattered little, however, but for the mil-itary communism of Sparta. This communism was necessar-ily based on regimentation rather than anarchy, given that the conquest was recent, that the Greek elite was a minority, and that fierce discipline was necessary in order to survive. This was a strange society, not least in the elite's practice of waging war on its own Helots once a year.[14] Nonetheless,

[13] D. Dawson, *Cities of the Gods* (Oxford: Oxford University Press, 1992).
[14] P. Cartledge, *The Spartans: The World of the Warrior-Heroes of Ancient Greece* (Woodstock, NY: Overlook Press, 2003).

Plato glorified Sparta, and his influence thereafter ensured a favorable hearing for the Spartan tradition.[15]

Far more important, however, than military communism was the sharing that occurred inside charismatic communities, a particularly clear example of which appears in the Acts of the Apostles:

All whose faith had drawn them together held everything in common: they would sell their property and possessions and make a general distribution as the need of each required. With one mind they kept up their daily attendance at the temple, and, breaking bread in private houses, shared their meals with unaffected joy, as they praised God and enjoyed the favour of the whole people. And day by day the Lord added to their number those whom he was saving.

The belief that the Second Coming was imminent makes this sharing comprehensible. The same consideration helps us understand the Taborites and several sects of Anabaptists, particularly those led by Jan Matthys and John of Leiden in Münster between 1534 and 1535.[16] Nonetheless, there are examples of communism existing without millenarian expectations. One type of such "normal" communism seeks to establish new and pure societies. This applies to the Carpocratians of second-century Egypt who chose to

[15] E. Rawson, *The Spartan Tradition in European Thought* (Oxford: Clarendon Press, 1969).

[16] N. Cohn, *The Pursuit of the Millenium: Revolutionary Millenarians and Mystical Anarchists of the Middle Ages*, 2nd ed. (New York: Harper Torchbooks, 1961).

expose the stupidity of earthly rules by systematic antinomianism. Still more striking were the Hutterites. Continual reinforcement of personnel within this group came from expulsion elsewhere, with measured discipline in the Bruderhof deriving from clerical rule. Even if this depended at all times on support from the Moravian nobility, it remains impressive that perhaps forty thousand people participated in a very severe form of communism. But there is a second variant within this general type, and it does not reject but rather works with established society. Monasticism represents differentiation, as Weber stressed, whereby a specialized elite renounces the world and lives in communist style. Such a division was probably necessary for medieval European society: primogeniture gave a rationale to monasticism by providing employment for younger sons. And Weber is probably right to stress that new attitudes to work derive more from monasticism than from primitive Christianity.

The third source of communist ideas and practices is that of isolated intellectuals. It is worth making a generalization here about the attraction of intellectuals to communist ideals, for in this matter we need to go beyond Durkheim's realization that dreamers produce such ideals to explaining why this should be so. In Plato's own case, modern scholarship has gone far in supporting Karl Popper's contention that Plato was attracted to a closed world as the result of a sheer dislike of the way in which the advent of democracy undermined the position of the aristocracy from which he sprang.[17] Similar displacements may explain the attraction

---

[17] K. R. Popper, *The Open Society and Its Enemies* (London: Routledge, 1945), supported by E. M. Wood and N. Wood, *Class Ideology and Ancient Political*

of other intellectuals to communism. This is most obviously the case with Thomas More, the most famous of all "idle dreamers." He had been deeply influenced by the monastic ethic, and in a sense disliked the secular world within which he had to operate. He is representative of a type of intellectual displaced by the Reformation's assault on monasticism.

The nature of premodern communism lends most support to Weber's social theory, although the last type identified—but not the reasons for its existence—derives from Durkheim. Two analytic points then force themselves upon us. First, communism in premodern circumstances was extremely rare. It requires a very considerable break in normal societal relations in order to institutionalize it. Conquest certainly creates a break of this sort, and it is this that explains the Jesuit communist communities in Paraguay quite as much as it does Sparta. Equally, millenarian expectations of religious charisma more generally so disrupt the normal as to induce social experimentation. The general point is reinforced by the aberrant case of early Iranian communism.[18] Here the sharing of women was suggested by a ruler, Kavadh I, who was keen to discipline his nobility; once the idea had been put into practice and the nobility weakened, its ideology then came to be adopted by Mazdak, the leader of a peasant revolt. Second, it is worth underscoring the fact that the examples of communism have been derived from the Occident. Muslim and Confucian societies did not share the Greek admiration for primitive peoples, because they

Theory (New York: Oxford University Press, 1978); but see, too, the cautionary words in Dawson, *Cities of the Gods*, chapter 2.

[18] P. Crone, "Kavad's Heresy and Mazdak's Revolt," *Iran* 29 (1991).

were utterly self-confident of their worth as civilizations, which makes examples of communist ideas and practices within these social worlds hard to find. The ethic of India is interestingly different, with renunciation taking a form that neither required nor involved sharing nor any sort of social organization.

Anthropology makes one aware of highly diverse social forms, with actions that seem strange to us making complete sense to those who inhabit these different realms. Nonetheless, some cultural patterns seem harder to maintain than others. Pure altruism is especially hard to maintain; this had been Montesquieu's argument, as noted, against the tradition of civic virtue. In particular, practices that make sense when the millennium is expected prove contentious once it is necessary to live within a continuing social world. This is not to deny that such practices can be maintained by a virtuous elite, as in monasticism or in a vanguard party, but it is to insist that whole societies have difficulty supporting such generalized heroism and enthusiasm for very long. There is a clear link here to the nature of communism in the modern world. The background consideration to bear in mind is the account, given in chapter 3, of the undoubted but idiosyncratic emergence of a politicized working class, the result of the autocratic regime with which Russian workers had to interact. This class helped make a revolution, but the revolution would probably never have taken place without the opportunity presented by the regime's defeat in war. After the heroic and brutal period of war, communism followed the period of the New Economic Plan, designed to secure the revolution by not disturbing social relations, especially in the countryside. Much of the radical intellectual elite hated this humdrum and boring world, wholly bereft of heroism. This elite embraced collectivization with enthusiasm once geopolitics suggested the need to build socialism quickly. Building something utterly new—a morally complete and economically productive society—was a world historical task that gave them a role, made almost more significant *because* it required the shedding of blood. Of course, hideous divisions among the elite then took place, leading to the purges and to the short period of genuine totalitarianism. Military victory then extended socialism. But slowly, normal politics and "normalization" processes after invasion made the people of the socialist bloc realize that they were living in a boring, shabby, and stagnant world. Accordingly, state socialist regimes can be judged to have placed excessive demands on their citizens: continual sharing requires too much effort. The revulsion to which this led could be seen in the total lack of interest in the "Swedish model" in the years immediately after 1989; any party then committed to socialism was doomed to electoral defeat.

But this claim does not take us all that far. For one thing, this general consideration does not explain why collapse took place at a particular moment, in 1989/1991, though it does help account for the weakness of attempts to recreate or restore the regime. Seeking an explanation requires recalling three general interpretations of state socialism. The first of these was totalitarianism. In authors such as Hannah Arendt, the revolutionary regime was seen as all-powerful, able at once to destroy existing social institutions and to rule effectively by means of sheer terror. The second position, modernization or liberalization, insisted that the moment of high totalitarianism had passed, and that a much more technocratic elite sought to gain the allegiance and cooperation of those key sectors of society that would help in economic development. Where these theories concentrated on elite politics, the third approach, which gained popularity in the 1980s tended to give priority to social forces operating from below. The notion of civil society, that is, of the increasing capacity of varied types of social groups to organize themselves in opposition to the state, was designed to address the fact that it was increasingly difficult for the party-state to arrange compacts between state and society.

For many years, good reasons existed for endorsing the second position. Central Europe was certainly a world without legitimacy, as was so graphically demonstrated in 1956, 1968, and 1981, and it seemed likely that it would somewhere, somehow, sooner or later change, essentially for social evolutionary reasons. The heroic period of Bolshevism had managed to industrialize, albeit in a brutal manner, but it was clearly proving to be less and less effective in economic terms everywhere, as a transition to more advanced levels of industrial society took place. The nature of computers seemed to make the point most effectively. Widespread possession of printers was surely necessary if society was to thrive in the late industrial era. But to accept this was to leave behind the days in which the attempt to break the bounds of censorship involved spreading samizdat documents produced by typing through several sheets of carbon paper at a time. Crucially, it was possible to see in most ruling parties a schizophrenic gap between technocrats and

Bolsheviks, between those who wished to give the party new life by assuring economic growth and those who were prepared to maintain socialism as an ideocracy, a power system based on an unsullied and unquestioned total ideology. In a sense, the moment in 1968 when Kádár, himself imposed upon by the Russians in 1956, announced that the rules of the system had changed—so that it would be enough simply not to oppose the system rather than having to endorse it enthusiastically at every moment—signaled the formal start of softer political rule. Liberalization was thus under way, and the era of high totalitarianism finished.

It seemed very likely that liberalization would continue. Modernizing leaders might be able to work with the technically competent, who had enough sense of international comparison to know that their mobility had been blocked, to create a more vigorous economy in tandem with softer political rule:

> An advanced industrial society requires a large scientific, technical, administrative, educational stratum, with genuine competence based on prolonged training. In other words, it cannot rely on rigid ideologies and servile classes alone. It is reasonable to assume that this kind of educated middle class, owing its position to technical competence rather than to subservience, and inherently, so to speak professionally, capable of distinguishing reality and thought from verbiage and incantation, will develop or has developed the kind of tastes we associate with its life-style—a need for security, a recognition of competence rather than subservi-

ence, a regard for efficiency and integrity rather than patronage and loyalty in professional life. . . . This class is large, and it cannot be penalized effectively without a cost to the economy which may no longer be acceptable.[19]

Great skill would be needed to make the most of favorable opportunity, to ask for reasonable change so that alliances could be made between frustrated, educated labor in society and technocrats inside the ruling elite; differently put, to ask too much too fast ran the risk of an endangered and re-unified elite calling in Russian tanks. Here there was an overlap with the burgeoning literature of the early 1980s on transitions from authoritarian capitalist rule. This literature stressed the need to make pacts so as to reassure the powerful that change would not take place at their expense. In particular, successful transitions from authoritarian capitalism have been those initiated and controlled from above; in contrast, transitions from below have fared badly.[20] Mere powerful societal self-organization would not be enough: civil self-restraint within oppositional groups was essential.

These considerations led me to a warm endorsement of the strategy adopted by Gorbachev. He seemed the perfect technocrat, keen to admit that he had been impressed by Western standards of consumption and with a wife whose abilities in that area were not open to question. One pre-

---

[19] E. Gellner, "Plaidoyer pour une Libéralisation Manquée," *Government and Opposition* 14 (1979): 63–64.
[20] T. Karl, "Dilemmas of Democratization in Latin America," *Comparative Politics* 23 (1990).

sumed that the attempt to reform must have received support from the leaders of the armed forces, and more probably from the military-industrial complex as a whole. Why else would such a conservative force allow reform? Most important, military spending had overstretched the Soviet Union and seriously impaired its economy. Crucially, it seemed as if this economic debilitation was beginning to have negative consequences even for the military. While skepticism may have been shown to the complete claims of Reagan's Star Wars initiative, the fear that American high technology would have military applications that could not be imitated was very real indeed. It was clear that Gorbachev's purpose was that of making the system work, but that pill was sugared by the prospect of softer political rule. Furthermore, by the late 1970s the geriatric and worried elite had perhaps lost its greatest virtue, that of the considerable circumspection that had been shown in foreign affairs. That Gorbachev seemed prepared not just to leave Afghanistan but to let Central Europe go turned endorsement into enthusiasm.

But liberalization failed. For a short period it seemed as if roundtable discussions leading to various types of pacts, habitually creating electoral rules designed to reassure the elite, were part of the classical scenario for controlled decompression. But this was merely a stage, and a very short one at that. What followed was an absolute and fundamental collapse. The long roundtable talks in Poland did produce rules designed to keep the party in power, but these were invalidated by the very first election. In general, what happened in Central Europe was that the removal of the Russian card meant that regimes simply crumbled. Once deprived of the capacity to repress their own people, party-states fell apart—with the notable exception of Romania, where much blood was spilled in the process of removing Ceauşescu.

Does this mean that we should accept the view from below? As it happens, the notion is far from clear, with striking differences being apparent between theorists in the West and in the East—the former hoping for new social movements to replace the proletariat, the latter often approving of the spread of capitalism. Nonetheless, there is some truth to the view from below. If civil society was a much-desired dream, the theory as a whole was not purely a matter of prescription. Solidarity provided the descriptive "beef" of the concept. This extraordinary movement, based on Christian mission and Polish destiny, changed the history of state socialism as a whole. Eastern Europe owed its freedom in part to the glorious Poles. It undermined the socialist project by leading to martial law, thereby removing any pretense that socialism was popular. That military rule was imposed by Poles rather than by Russian tanks presumably reflected the Kremlin's calculation that the Poles would have been prepared to engage in armed struggle, whatever the cost. Furthermore, it seems that increasing corruption—clientelism, nepotism, and patronage, in addition to sheer graft—did quite as much to discredit the regimes in their last decade.

But if the view from below has some truth, its general direction misleads. Most obviously, Solidarity had been controlled by the mid-1980s, albeit at very great cost in terms of legitimacy, while no other regime was threatened from below. Additionally, the lack of positive new initiatives should not be taken to mean that socialist regimes were bound to break down: a very long and messy period of "muddling through" would surely have been possible before unfavorable social trends gained real bite. It is important to recall that collapse, when it came, was like that of a house of cards, with events in one place imitating those in another at ever greater speed. Once Russian control had been withdrawn, as it was when the Kremlin allowed Hungary to open its borders to East Germans who wanted to go to the West, the regimes of 1945 began to crumble. In general, forces from below did not so much cause collapse as occupy political space once it became available.

If none of the three theories identified works well, we must ask why liberalization failed in the crucial case of the Soviet Union. While errors of judgment were certainly made, the fundamental reason why liberalization could not work in socialist society was that civil society had been destroyed.[21] States throughout history have been nervous about channels of communication that they can scarcely see. Accordingly, it has been very common to find that states ban horizontal linkages in society so as to privilege their own official means of communication. The reply of Trajan to Pliny (when he was the governor of Bithynia-Pontus) in response to his query as to whether to allow local organization of a fire brigade in Nicomedia is revealing: such organization should not even be contemplated, the emperor insisted, for once gathered together minds will drift from fires

---

[21] R. Bova, "Political Dynamics of the Post-Communist Transition: A Comparative Perspective," *World Politics* 121 (1991).

to politics.[22] In fact, in the long run, perhaps because of the cosmopolitanism inherent in its empire, Rome could not contain those horizontal channels of Christians to which it had reacted so harshly—and so eventually chose to accept what it could not control.[23] In contrast, China did perfect low-intensity rule in the agrarian era. The spirit of such rule, its preference for control at the expense of mobilized efficiency, was well understood by Tocqueville, who was well versed in the dead hand of French colonialism.[24] But to be fair, one must note that the destruction of independent groups in Russia owes as much to autocracy as to totalitarianism. Czarism had been as suspicious of civil society as it was opposed to capitalism and the rule of law: what mattered was the possibility of isolated individuals being able to approach their Great Father.[25] As is so often the case, revolution merely intensified existing social patterns: secret police, government inspectors, atomization, boredom, and privatization were familiar to late nineteenth-century Russians, albeit in infinitely milder form. Whatever the exact contribution of socialism rather than autocracy, there can be no doubt of the sterility, together with the weakness it caused, that was characteristic of socialist society. Not the least im-

---

[22] The exchange is in Pliny, *Pliny the Younger: Complete Letters*, trans. P. G. Walsh (Oxford: Oxford University Press, 2006), book 10, letters 33 and 34, 254–55.

[23] M. Mann, *Sources of Social Power*, vol. 1, *A History of Power from the Beginning to A.D. 1760* (Cambridge: Cambridge University Press, 1986), chapter 10.

[24] A. de Tocqueville, *The Old Regime and the French Revolution*, trans. S. Gilbert (New York: Anchor, 1955), 64.

[25] T. McDaniel, *Autocracy, Capitalism and Revolution in Russia* (Berkeley: University of California Press, 1988).

portant problem was that those who might have been reformers were turned into dissidents, with inner emigration depriving state socialism of basic energy.

The literature on transitions to democracy depends completely on the striking of bargains, above all, of a reforming elite seeking to give a little, to receive in return a signal that this has been understood and accepted, so that more can be given without fear of any complete loss of position. What is necessary is a partnership in which forces from below discipline themselves so as to reassure those at the top. But Eastern Europe was not Latin America. Though the theory of totalitarianism exaggerated the powers of the state, it was right when stressing the destruction of civil society. Liberalization was accordingly never really possible in the Soviet Union: the absence of partners in society made orderly decompression impossible. The key analytic point to be made about institutions is that they control as much as express social forces, thereby allowing the regulation of conflict by means of rational bargaining. A further interesting speculation has suggested that the absence of discipline at the bottom reflects more than the simple destruction of civil society. Had forces at the top been organized and united, the threat of their return to power might have been so obvious as to create some discipline in society. But the elite was not at all like that. Very much to the contrary, party members— at least in some countries, most notably Hungary—had clearly decided before 1989 that the most secure route to privilege was through the economy rather than through political position.

A final point needs to be made about liberalization and

collapse. One of Tocqueville's great insights was that liberalization was difficult, that the moment of reform was that of
the greatest potential weakness. Expectations tend to increase, and to run ahead of the ability to deliver them: the
paradox is that the new regime may fall, even though it is
more legitimate than the old one. Certainly Gorbachev felt
these pressures. But he was by no means, as Western commentators imagined, the skillful master politician, making
the best of the small amount or room in which to maneuver.
The worst possible conduct during any liberalization process, as Tocqueville stressed when examining the policies of
Louis XVI, is to dither. To raise expectations and then to
dash them virtually inspires revolutionary feelings in ener-
gized people. What is necessary is consistency: a clear and
absolute outlining of priorities, a listing of areas where
change is permissible and where it is not, and fierce determination not to retreat from announced reform when difficulties arise. It is necessary, in other words, to take the long
view, to realize that an increase in liberalism will eventually
diffuse conflict: in the politics of decompression, it is vital
to do what one announces and to be sparing in what one
promises.

It was particularly mad illogic on Gorbachev's part to
offer much to the Baltic states, and then to threaten them.
This is to say that the nationalities problem was partly created by Gorbachev. The legacy of distrust in the Soviet empire was, of course, extremely high, and any move to greater
openness was likely to be treated with skepticism. But this
meant that the only route for success lay through greater

rather than lesser boldness. Early calling of union elections, which Gorbachev could not stomach, was vital.[26] To say this returns us to the question of democracy. Was not democratization rather than liberalization inevitable if the nationalities question was to be solved? It is crucial to make a distinction. There is a great difference between democratization that follows collapse and democratization willingly given so as to ensure the continuity of structures that may thereby be shored up. Voluntary renunciation of power enables more of it to be retained: in other words, a firm, planned move toward elections could have been part of a liberalization strategy. In this sense, the handling of the nationalities question was the worst possible. There might have been logic to letting the Baltic states go and in being strict elsewhere; what was disastrous was to pretend to be tough to the Baltics and then to let them go, thereby giving occasion and precedent to other regions where nationalism to that point had been rather weak. This gave Yeltsin his cards, which he then played with consummate skill so as to destroy his great rival. One irony (among many others) deserves underscoring. In one sense, it was fortunate that proper sociological understanding was *not* available. That totalitarianism had so destroyed civil society as to rule out any careful decompression amounts to saying that it was nearly inevitable that socialist leaders would lose control. Had this been known in advance, it would have encouraged such bunker mentality that no change would have been attempted. Put differently,

[26] J. Linz and A. Stepan, "Political Identities and Electoral Sequences: Spain, the Soviet Union and Yugoslavia," *Daedalus* 121 (1992).

Gorbachev destroyed state socialism because he was blind. He did everything that Tocqueville warned against, and thereby became a veritable angel of destruction.

One concluding thought presses itself forward. Chinese communism has weathered the storm of the past years. Perestroika before glasnost may increase the chances of liberalization by creating partners with whom the state may eventually be able to work. But is it still communist?

CHAPTER 9

The Destruction of Trust

The analysis of trust has become a central focus in contemporary social theory. This is wholly to be welcomed, for it takes but a moment to realize that social life depends on trust. Parents and children habitually rely on each other without much question, with an enormous amount being simply taken for granted. Cooperative relations in general depend on trust, on the expectation that agreements will be honored. One example of this is the agreement to differ, the subject of chapter 1. So civility rests on trust. Accordingly, those who destroy trust must be ranked as enemies of civility. Alexis de Tocqueville's account of such enemies is unduly neglected given its immense intellectual power. And it matters very greatly to the argument of this book, as it makes us turn our attention to the state.

Tocqueville seems to me to be the greatest of all theorists of trust.[1] This claim can be specified; it should not be misunderstood. "I have only one passion," Tocqueville declared in 1837 in a letter to Henry Reeve, "the love of liberty and human dignity. All forms of government are in my eyes only

---

[1] Good use of Tocqueville is made by G. Hawthorn, "Three Ironies in Trust," in *Trust: Making and Breaking Cooperative Relations*, ed. D. Gambetta (Oxford: Basil Blackwell, 1988).

more or less perfect ways of satisfying this holy and legitimate passion of man."[2] Differently put, no radical claim is
being made here to the effect that Tocqueville is a sociologist
of trust *rather* than of liberty; the claim is simply that what
Tocqueville did have to say about trust in political life is exceedingly high-powered, and of particular interest in a period in which many attempts to create or to restore cooperative relations are being made. It is not, of course, surprising
that his ideas about trust are so impressive once we understand that there are several affinities between trust and liberty. Tocqueville has much to tell us about psychological and
institutional links between trust and liberty, and pleasure
can be derived from reconstructing his views. Tocqueville's
views of a world without trust are especially striking. The
central thesis maintained here is that Tocqueville changed
his mind about the circumstances that caused the loss of
trust. The position at which he arrived is one in which kings
rather than people are blamed for the loss of trust in society.
In my view, Tocqueville's final position is not just more powerful but actually correct: if intellectuals can be dangerous,
political elites are still more likely to undermine civility.

   Without further ado, let me turn to Tocqueville's view of
a world without trust. It is important to appreciate that
Tocqueville regarded the possibility of a democratic tyranny
of the majority with visceral dread and fear. Much more was
involved here than such facets of the democratic era as the
distaste for great men and noble literary themes. Tocque-

---

[2] A. de Tocqueville, *Selected Letters on Politics and Society*, ed. R. Boesche, trans.
J. Toupin and R. Boesche (Berkeley: University of California Press, 1985), 115.

ville had been deeply influenced by Pascal and Rousseau, and accordingly believed that men could be subject to base and depraved passions quite as much as to more noble feelings. In particular, he believed that human beings had within them a devil that once released could make social and political life sheer hell. The passion in question—envy—is not always properly understood. In particular, it is crucial to recall the difference between jealousy and envy. Jealousy leads an individual who is aware that someone else has something, including the affections of another person, to imitate and copy: it is a positive and vitalizing emotion—with links to trust—that encourages the individual to reach higher in order to achieve. Envy is exactly the opposite.[3] Its central core received inimitable treatment in Shakespeare's *Othello*: when Iago realizes that there is a beauty in Cassio's life that makes his ugly, his response is not to emulate the handsome Florentine but to destroy him. Envy is the evil eye that seeks not to imitate but to pull down: the destruction of a quality or a person removes the offense. It is this passion that Tocqueville feared would be released by modern circumstances. At best, the release of envy would remove all distinction. At worst, Tocqueville felt that there was a natural fit between despotism and social equality: rather than allow difference and divergence, the many would prefer to suffer in common, to be equal under a single ruler.

The initial presupposition of Tocqueville's thought is that the advent of democracy was responsible for releasing

[3] H. Schoeck, *Envy: A Theory of Social Behavior*, trans. M. Glenny and B. Ross (New York: Harcourt, 1969).

this passion. To hold such a view was entirely characteristic of a whole generation of French intellectuals.[4] Generalized dislike was shown to the individualism encouraged by bourgeois society, together with premonitions as to the political consequences of the isolation that its social form encouraged. Tocqueville insisted that individualism was a modern concept, "unknown to our ancestors, for the good reason that in their days every individual necessarily belonged to a group and no one could regard himself as an isolated unit."[5] Such individualism began by encouraging a retreat into private life, only then to create a form of egoism opposed to all public spirit.[6] This was naturally anathema to Tocqueville given his allegiance to the republican tradition of civic virtue.[7] If Tocqueville took that from Rousseau, he was as much influenced by Montesquieu, accepting his view that liberty naturally characterized aristocratic circumstances. Liberty was guaranteed by the presence of competing groups, each one of which generated powerful ties of mutual loyalty and support. Perhaps a shared aristocratic background explains their insistence that self-

[4] R. Boesche, *The Strange Liberalism of Alexis de Tocqueville* (Ithaca: Cornell University Press, 1987), part 1.

[5] Tocqueville, *The Old Regime and the French Revolution*, 96.

[6] A. de Tocqueville, *Democracy in America* (1835 and 1840), trans. H. C. Mansfield and D. Winthrop (Chicago: Chicago University Press, 2000), 514–17. Cf. J. C. Lamberti, *Tocqueville et les deux democraties* (Paris: Presses Universitaires de France, 1970).

[7] On this tradition, see J.G.A. Pocock, *The Machiavellian Moment* (Princeton: Princeton University Press, 1975). For an appreciation of Tocqueville's allegiance to this tradition in comparison to thinkers who endorsed bourgeois society without major qualification, see A. O. Hirschman, *The Passions and the Interests: Political Arguments for Capitalism before Its Triumph* (Princeton: Princeton University Press, 1977).

restraint and self-mastery were necessary if liberty was to be sustained.

But if Tocqueville shared much with his generation, he also chose to differ from it. In private life, he opposed the dictates of his family and married a middle-class English-woman.[8] In political affairs, he chose to serve the bourgeois republic of Louis Philippe—against the wishes not just of his father but also of his class. This decision to adapt to the new order explains his interest in the United States: by examining the most advanced of all democracies, Tocqueville felt he would be able to say something about France's likely future.

It is important at this point to be more precise than was Tocqueville himself about his exact intellectual concern. Confusion has been caused by the different connotations attached to the concept of democracy. Tocqueville takes democracy to be a new era of equal social conditions. As his ultimate value is liberty, the central theme of his thought can in fact be simply stated. What will be the politics of the era of equality of conditions? Will this new age be characterized by arbitrary rule or by the presence of political liberty? And would it be possible, when people are so similar, to prevent a more thoroughgoing despotism than ever before?

The first volume of *Democracy in America* produced a favorable report on the United States. Tocqueville was *surprised* to discover that political liberty and equal social conditions could coexist. He confided to his travel journal his contempt for the middle classes, noting, almost reluctantly,

---

[8] For details, see A. Jardin's excellent *Tocqueville* (New York: Farrar, Straus and Giroux, 1988).

that "in spite of their petty passions, their incomplete education and their vulgar manners, they clearly can provide practical intelligence."[9] Let us examine in turn the three factors—accidental, legal, and cultural—by means of which the United States reached its happy condition.

The most important accident allowing the United States to be at once equal and free is provided by geography:

> The Americans have no neighbours and consequently no great wars, financial crises, ravages, or conquest to fear; they need neither large taxes, nor a numerous army, nor great generals; they have almost nothing to dread from a scourge more terrible for republics than all those things put together—military glory.[10]

This point can be put in slightly different terms: the creation of a powerful state apparatus makes it hard to maintain liberty. The United States was saved from this fate by geographical isolation from the major centers of interstate conflict. But other accidental factors are also considered to have played a part. Most important, abundance of land allowed for the egalitarian spirit of the early settlers to be maintained: no hierarchy could be easily created given that a laborer could always move on toward the frontier. In these circumstances, acquisitiveness did not breed corruption: on the contrary, the ability to extract plenty from the land

[9] A. de Tocqueville, *Journey to America*, ed. J. P. Mayer, trans. G. Lawrence, rev. ed. in collaboration with A. P. Kerr (New York: Anchor, 1971), 259, cited by Boesche, *The Strange Liberalism of Alexis de Tocqueville*, 89.
[10] Tocqueville, *Democracy in America*, 265.

depended on knowledge and independence, thereby creating the benefits of prosperity that helped to maintain the Republic.

Second, liberty was maintained by means of the laws. Tocqueville has much of interest to say about the judicial system, particularly about its capacity to restrain sudden outbursts of feeling. But of greater import here are his comments about participation. Tocqueville stresses that the American Constitution managed to combine the benefits of a great power at one and the same time as it allows the involvement characteristic of smaller societies. The United States, in another of Tocqueville's formulations, possesses executive centralization with administrative decentralization. One benefit of this is that the United States is not dominated by a great capital. But of absolutely central importance is the fact that a decentralized system allows people to engage in politics. Tocqueville was impressed by the political participation he observed in New England, and he suggested that it served as a bulwark against the tyranny of the majority.[11] When people are actively engaged in political life, they begin to appreciate the benefits of hearing differences of opinion; equally, they gain both a taste for freedom and the necessary skills to maintain it. Liberty depends upon the civic training that can come only from taking charge of one's destiny. Cooperation between classes and in-

[11] Tocqueville's admiration for New England town meetings was, in a sense, overdone. G. W. Pierson, *Tocqueville and Beaumont in America* (New York: Oxford University Press, 1938) makes it clear that by the 1830s—in the midst of Jackson's presidency!—New England was no longer a guide to the complete political reality of the United States.

dividuals is relatively easy to achieve within such a world, and this amounts to Tocqueville's genealogy of trust. His general position is made particularly clear in a passage disputing the claim that the state needs to become more skillful and active in proportion as the citizens become weaker and more helpless:

> Sentiments and ideas renew themselves, the heart is enlarged, and the human mind is developed only by the reciprocal action of men upon one another.[12]

For Tocqueville, a state can only truly be powerful if it is in a relationship of trust with its citizens—an idea that, as we will see, became central to his later work.

The third type of general cause concerns what Tocqueville felicitously called "the habits of the heart." Here Tocqueville's argument goes very much against current preconceptions in insisting that it is respect for religion that underlies liberty in the United States. One part of his argument is particularly clear and strikingly sociologically perceptive. He suggests that freeing the church from state control will encourage the spread of religious faith: in other words, secularization is usually at least half a political movement; that is, it is occasioned by the need to attack the strengthening of the politically powerful by religious legitimation. Altogether harder to understand, however, is the core of Tocqueville's argument: that religion is necessary for liberty because it places some limits on human behavior. It is worth quoting Tocqueville at some length on

---

[12] Tocqueville, *Democracy in America*, 491.

this point. After explaining that the general respect for religion supports family life, he notes:

> The imagination of Americans in its greatest leaps has therefore only a circumspect and uncertain step; its pace is hindered and its works are incomplete. These habits of restraint are to be found in political society and singularly favour the tranquillity of the people as well as the longevity of the institutions it has given itself. Nature and circumstances have made the inhabitant of the United States an audacious man; it is easy to judge of this when one sees the manner in which he pursues his fortune. If the spirit of the Americans were free of all impediments, one would soon encounter among them the boldest innovators and the most implacable logicians in the world. But revolutionaries in America are obliged to profess openly a certain respect for the morality and equity of Christianity, which does not permit them to violate its laws easily when they are opposed to the execution of their designs; and if they could raise themselves above their own scruples, they would still feel they were stopped by those of their partisans. Up to now, no one has been encountered in the United States who dared to advance the maxim that everything is permitted in the interest of society. An impious maxim—one that seems to have been invented in a century of freedom to legitimate all the tyrants to come.[13]

---

[13] Ibid., 279–80.

This passage offers, in my opinion, a very powerful insight into American political culture, but it needs, nonetheless, some highlighting. Tocqueville's oeuvre as a whole suggests that what is at issue here is not in fact very complex. When we recall that the devil in modern political behavior is envy, it becomes apparent that the key self-limitation imposed by religion results from it regarding that passion as sinful. Religious belief entails respect for the gifts bestowed on humanity by God. What do differences between men matter given the much larger fact of equality in the sight of God?

Tocqueville's contemporaries, as well as subsequent critics, have found the second volume of *Democracy in America* less forceful than the first, despite its obvious felicities. What is noticeable here is that Tocqueville can be seen as beginning to doubt his basic argument, that it is equal social conditions that create envy and thereby encourage despotism. His chapter "Why Democratic Nations Show a More Ardent and Enduring Love for Equality than for Liberty" begins by being true to its title. But toward the end of the chapter, the target of the discussion subtly changes:

> Democratic peoples love equality at all times, but in certain periods, they press the passion they feel for it to delirium. This happens at the moment when the old social hierarchy, long threatened, is finally destroyed after a last internecine struggle. . . .
>
> What precedes applies to all democratic nations. What follows regards only us.
>
> In most modern nations and in particular in all the peoples of the continent of Europe, the taste for and

idea of freedom began to arise and to develop only at the moment when conditions began to be equalized and as a consequence of that very equality. It was the absolute kings who worked the most at levelling the ranks among their subjects. In these peoples, equality preceded freedom; equality was therefore an old fact when freedom was still a new thing; the one had already created opinions, usages, laws proper to it when the other was produced alone and for the first time in broad daylight. Thus the latter existed still only in ideas and tastes, whereas the former had already penetrated habits, taken hold of mores, and given a particular turn to the least acts of life.[14]

It is this line of argument that is fully developed in *The Old Regime and the French Revolution*, to which we can turn after making one important prefatory point.

In the most general terms, what is noticeable about the United States is that it was a cultural offshoot of England. It was created with equal social conditions and political liberty; it was born free. This renders Tocqueville's analysis essentially static: it is an examination of social and political institutions that counterbalance the tendency, inherent in a society of equal social conditions, toward the tyranny of the majority. The essentially cheerful report that Tocqueville issues on the United States is consequently of limited use when it comes to understanding Europe. European society had the social hierarchy created by a feudal past, and the na-

---

[14] Ibid., 481–82.

ture of the transition that the various national states make toward the world of equal social conditions therefore becomes absolutely vital. If Tocqueville's central problem—how can liberty and equal social conditions be combined—remains the same, a key part of the agenda now becomes the *historical development* of both these forces. So let us turn from the striking book that he wrote when young to his masterpiece, *The Old Regime and the French Revolution*.

We know that in the 1850s Tocqueville had originally attempted to produce an analysis of the failure of France to embrace political liberty in the years after 1848—a failure that drove him to the depths of despair.[15] That remained his question: the central subject of the book is the propensity of France to embrace despotism. But in seeking to understand why this was the case, Tocqueville was driven backward in time; he found the explanation less in modern social circumstances than in the nature of the Old Regime. Outlining his account must be our initial task. But Tocqueville's argument gains very considerable force because he has—half implicitly, half explicitly—two control groups. He devotes an appendix to Languedoc, an area of France that resisted most of the centralizing encroachments of the absolutist regime, and had, in consequence, a very different social physiognomy. Far more important are the comments made about England, a society with a feudal past that nonetheless possesses liberty in the era of equal social conditions. Tocqueville is one of the greatest of France's Anglophiles, and the

[15] R. Herr, *Tocqueville and the Old Regime* (Princeton: Princeton University Press, 1962).

English comparison serves as a foil for French developments at every step of his argument.

Tocqueville was a far more systematic thinker than is often realized. When dealing with France and England, he asked about the same types of social cause that had structured his account of the United States: namely, accidents, laws, and mores or habits of the heart. We can follow him in using these categories, though clarity of presentation will be enhanced by taking them in an order different from that used when dealing with the United States. Let us begin with the laws of France.

Tocqueville tells us that what surprised him most in the research for his book was the discovery that administrative centralization was the work of the Old Regime rather than of the Revolution. Several aspects of this centralization may be traced. The absolutist regime placed its own servants, the intendants, in every area of France so as to rule and tax through them. Even where old systems of authority were left, they were effectively undermined. Thus, court cases that presented difficulties for the regime were "called" to Paris. Furthermore, the autonomy of towns was destroyed by Richelieu, that of the aristocracy by Louis XIV. The latter built Versailles so as to neuter his aristocracy by removing them from their power bases and placing them under his supervision. The consequences of all these changes were profound. Most obviously, the administration learned to distrust the people:

> Any independent group, however small, which seemed desirous of taking action otherwise than under the

aegis of the administration filled it with alarm, and the
tiniest free association of citizens, however harmless
its aims, was regarded as a nuisance. The only corporate bodies tolerated were those whose members had
been hand-picked by the administration and which
were under its control. Even big industrial concerns
were frowned upon. In a word, our administration resented the idea of private citizens' having any say in the
control of their own enterprises, and preferred sterility
to competition.[16]

In general, the administration realized that its power was
negative, resting as it did on preventing linkages between
the people that it could not oversee: it was able to control
but not to mobilize the people. And the people, bereft of
the chances of participation, increasingly looked to the
state for social improvements, and came to regard it almost
as a deity in its own right. In these circumstances, Parisian
affairs began to have a profound effect on French politics as
a whole.

Administrative centralization was but one side of the picture of laws and institutions. The most brilliant pages in all
of Tocqueville are contained in chapters 8–10 of the second
part of the book. The first of these three chapters explains
"How France had become the country in which men were
most like each other." What was involved here, in Tocqueville's view and in that of later historians whose work supports this point, was the convergence of income levels and

[16] Tocqueville, *The Old Regime and the French Revolution*, 64.

lifestyles of the aristocracy and the bourgeoisie.[17] The second stage of the argument is a nice example of Tocqueville's love of paradox: chapter 9 considers "How, though in many respects so similar, the French were split up more than ever before into small, isolated, self-regarding groups." This section begins with an analysis of local politics before the advent of absolutism. Records showed that classes had once been able to trust each other, and to cooperate with each other in defending regional interests. This spirit of class cooperation was shattered most of all by the granting of tax and legal immunities to the French aristocracy: this destroyed all community of interest, and naturally made it senseless to serve as leaders against the encroachments of the state. This basic separation of the classes was exacerbated by the state raising extra revenues by granting more special privileges. This was so excessive that it not only set bourgeois against aristocrat but some sections within the bourgeoisie against many of their colleagues. The final stage in the argument, chapter 10, bluntly considers "the suppression of political freedom and the barriers set up between classes." It is here that Tocqueville finds an explanation for France's inability to combine equal social conditions with political liberty. The exercise of political liberty depends, as noted, upon trust between different social classes, while it in turn breeds responsibility; differently put, participation is the only effective means of training citizens suited to liberty. The trouble with the pattern of the French past, in contrast, is that envy has been so encouraged by rulers as to make peo-

---

[17] P. Higonnet, *Class, Ideology and the Rights of Nobles during the French Revolution* (New York: Oxford University Press, 1981).

ple prefer equality under a despot to differentiation under liberty. The whole burden of Tocqueville's argument is thus to offer a political explanation for the rise of envy and destruction of trust. His own summary on this point is brutal:

> Almost all the vices, miscalculations and disastrous prejudices I have been describing owed their origin, their continuance, and their proliferation to a line of conduct practised by so many of our Kings, that of dividing men so as the better to rule them.[18]

Tocqueville had changed his mind about the loss of trust. Liberty is undermined less by passions released by the age of social conditions and much more by those created by the strategy of the state.

Let us complete Tocqueville's argument. The analysis of the "habits of the heart" of French people is well known, both because it became a staple of nineteenth-century French social thought and because it gave rise to a striking thesis by Daniel Mornet on the intellectual origins of the French Revolution.[19] Three critical and mutually reinforcing points are made by Tocqueville about the political culture of eighteenth-century France. First, the divide-and-rule strategy of the absolutist state meant that the intellectuals, quite as much as other social actors, lost touch with political reality. They criticized society remorselessly, heedless of social costs, and produced plans that looked perfect on the drawing

[18] Tocqueville, *The Old Regime and the French Revolution*, 136.
[19] D. Mornet, *Les origines intellectuelles de la Revolution francaise, 1715–1787* (Paris : A Colin, 1933).

board but were to prove extremely dangerous in practice. Second, particularly important in this regard was their assault on religion. Tocqueville explains this assault in terms familiar from his earlier book: it was the alliance of church and state that led to anticlericalism. That attack was, he stresses, exceedingly dangerous because it removed all limits from politics: when everything is possible, in Tocqueville's eyes, despotism becomes likely. Third, Tocqueville notes that a particular group of intellectuals, the economists, much preferred order to liberty. The Physiocrats sought to make the state enlightened and despotic, unaware, in Tocqueville's eyes, that what was really necessary was a diminution of the presence of the state. A general point is called for at this point. Tocqueville is telling us that intellectuals become enemies of civility because of political exclusion; this is one reason for suggesting that civility is endangered most of all by the behavior of states.

The central comment made about accidental causes is a neat counterpoint to the isolation of the United States. The fundamental origin of the absolutist state in France lies in an institutional change introduced at the blackest moment of the Hundred Years' War with England:

It was on the day when the French people, weary of the chaos into which the kingdom had been plunged for so many years by the captivity of King John and the madness of Charles VI, permitted the King to impose a tax without their consent and the nobles showed so little public spirit as to connive at this, provided their own immunity was guaranteed—it was on that fateful

day that the seeds were sown of almost all the vices
and abuses which led to the violent downfall of the old
regime.[20]

The basis of class cooperation had been respect for the two
maxims of canon law that had governed representative estates; namely, "no taxation without representation" and
"what touches all must be agreed by all."[21] Once these maxims were undermined, the state could divide society and
perch despotically on top of those divisions.

Before contrasting this portrait with those of Languedoc
and England, the nature of the case that Tocqueville has
made can usefully be highlighted. We are really being told
that history—and not, as Freud had it, biology—is destiny.
France lost its freedom under the Old Regime and is thus
basically incapable of having liberty in the new age of social
conditions. It is not, in other words, the actual process of
transition to equal conditions that matters; rather, patterns
of political organization and culture persist across social
transformations—a general ethic that also applies to England, as we shall see in a moment. This is a highly deter-
ministic conclusion, one that is wholly depressing.

Languedoc had been able to resist the centralizing ten-
dencies of the monarchy, and Tocqueville applauds the decision of the notables of Languedoc to collect taxes locally—
and this despite the fact that their total tax burden was
heavier. Running one's own affairs allowed trust in society

---

[20] Tocqueville, *The Old Regime and the French Revolution*, 98–99.
[21] A. R. Myers, *Parliaments and Estates in Europe to 1789* (London: Harcourt,
Brace, Jovanovich, 1975).

to continue; much is made of cooperation between classes. It is at this point that Tocqueville most clearly spells out an important theoretical point about the nature of state power. What he notes about Languedoc is that it was better governed than the rest of France. A lessening of despotism/retention of local liberties increased the rate of fiscal extraction because the aristocracy contributed to a government that it could control. In consequence of this, and of the greater knowledge created by trust in contrast to the power standoff characteristic of the rest of France, the level of social infrastructure and general prosperity was strikingly high. Constitutionalism breeds trust, and trust empowers. And this is true more generally of England as compared to France: for Tocqueville what matters about England is that its state is far more powerful than that of France, despite— or, rather *because of*—its lack of absolutist powers.[22]

England provides a neat counterpoint to France at each theoretical juncture on which Tocqueville's thought concentrates, and it equally forms a coherent and comprehensible whole. Tocqueville himself writes most extensively about the laws and institutions of England. What impresses him most is the resilience of the aristocracy. That resilience is explained by continuing social function: the lack of centralized state administration meant that the aristocrats provided local government. As in Languedoc, the aristocracy was not exempt from taxation, with the English state accordingly being strengthened by large revenues; hence,

---

[22] J. A. Hall, *Powers and Liberties: The Causes and Consequences of the Rise of the West* (Oxford: Basil Blackwell, 1985), chapter 5. Cf. J. Brewer, *The Sinews of War* (New York: Alfred A. Knopf, 1989).

aristocrats joined with other members of the community in resisting any extension of arbitrary state power. Both a consequence and a cause of this happy situation was the openness of the English upper classes. In France, privileges, legal and fiscal, had turned the aristocracy into a caste separate from the rest of society. In England, the absence of such privileges encouraged intermarriage and allowed the aristocracy to be opinion leaders for the whole of society. The success of that leadership was seen, for Tocqueville, in the way in which the idea of the gentleman became popular throughout society.

Tocqueville's comments about English geopolitics and the habits of the heart are less developed, albeit the contrast with France at each point is exceedingly neat. Geopolitically, England has the advantage of being an island, far less fearful of invasion and accordingly with citizens less likely to hand over their liberties because of the pains of war. Furthermore, Tocqueville is encouraging us to say simply that the presence of naval forces, rather than of a standing army, encourages liberty.[23] In more general matters of political culture, Tocqueville notes that English intellectuals are far less prone to create wild schemes because they have practical experience of political life. This is certainly an accurate description of the world of Hume and Smith, the theorists of empiricism and capitalism, both of whom sought to encourage prudence, calculation, and moderation. It is not, of course, true to say that these figures were themselves advocates of religion. Nonetheless, both Hume and Smith

[23] Cf. B. Moore, *Social Origins of Dictatorship and Democracy: Lord and Peasant in the Making of the Modern World* (Boston: Beacon Press, 1966).

sought, as noted, to discourage enthusiasm of any sort—
Hume by showing a decent respect for the dead certainties
of established religion, Smith by encouraging an increase of
religious sects that were able to balance and to check each
other.[24] For the sake of completeness, it is well worth noting
that one of the later members of the liberal and Anglophile
school of thought to which Tocqueville belongs can sensibly
be seen as completing his thought at this point. The first volume of Élie Halévy's celebrated history of England in the
nineteenth century offered an explanation for the relative
moderation of the working class in England as compared to
that of France during the course of the century.[25] Those at-
tacking the upper orders in France became by necessity anticlerical, with all the increase in radicalism—in this case toward Marxism—that superimposition of conflicts normally
imposes.[26] Such a course of action was not necessary in England. The partial disestablishment of the church meant
that the working class did not need to attack religion per se:
on the contrary, it could invent its own. The moderation
and organization of the British working class in the nineteenth century is to be ascribed in large part to its being
methodist rather than Marxist.

[24] D. Hume, *The Natural History of Religion* ([1757] Stanford, CA: Stanford
University Press, 1956); A. Smith, *An Inquiry into the Nature and Causes of the
Wealth of Nations*, book 5.

[25] É. Halévy, *A History of the English People in the Nineteenth Century*, vol. 1,
England in 1815, trans. E. I. Watkin ([1913] London: T. F. Unwin, 1934) and
The Birth of Methodism in England, trans. B. Semmel ([1906] Chicago: Univer-
sity of Chicago Press, 1971).

[26] The importance of superimposition is stressed by R. Dahrendorf, *Class and
Class Conflict in Industrial Society* (Stanford, CA: Stanford University Press,
1959).

Let me summarize and conclude. State behavior can destroy, thereby undermining civility. The principal argument
about Tocqueville is that he came ever more powerfully to
blame kings rather than people for the loss of trust within
society. This is a matter of great import. Majorities can
threaten minorities, but elites can repress and divide majorities into suspicious and warring groups. Accordingly, it is
best to see democracy as a necessary condition for civility in
modern times, even though sufficiency to that end requires
the creation and maintenance of a civil political culture.
Furthermore, Tocqueville has sometimes been utilized by
conservatives who wish to argue that the "socialistic envy"
of the people is both vile and a danger to settled contemporary capitalism. There is everything wrong with such a view.
Most obviously, it is not correct. Tocqueville's concern with
state-centered explanation can helpfully be seen, to begin
with, as lying at the back of an important, recent breakthrough in understanding the rise of socialism. There is now
something of a general agreement among political sociologists, as we saw in chapter 3, to the effect that socialist militancy was not created by the capitalist mode of production
but rather by ruling-class strategies. And the whole spirit of
Tocqueville's work stresses the possibility of working coop-
eratively—that is, of transcending material interests reduc-
tively defined. Contemporary historical sociology underlines the importance of this point when demonstrating that
European social democracy has depended on cross-class alliances—most obviously, those between peasants and workers in Scandinavia.[27]

---

[27] G. Esping-Anderson, *Politics against Markets: The Social Democratic Road to
Power* (Princeton: Princeton University Press, 1985).

Further points can be made against the conservative use of Tocqueville by considering *Habits of the Heart*, the most celebrated recent analysis of the character of American society produced by Robert Bellah and his colleagues. The authors of treatise should not be allowed to get away with their attempted appropriation of Tocqueville for their argument that American society should be reformed through reinforcing community sentiment at the expense of individualism.[28] Most immediately, Tocqueville was a pessimist, reluctant to concede that reform was ever likely to succeed. His analyses of the difficulties involved in liberalization are, of course, subtle and quite well known. His crucial point is that the envy encouraged by the Old Regime made cooperation impossible once it fell:

> It was no easy task bringing together fellow citizens who had lived for many centuries aloof from, or even hostile to, each other and teaching them to co-operate in the management of their own affairs. It had been far easier to estrange them than it now was to reunite them, and in so doing France gave the world a memorable example. Yet, when sixty years ago the various classes which under the old order had been isolated units in the social system came once again in touch, it was on their sore spots that they made contact and their first gesture was to fly at each other's throats. In-

---

[28] R. Bellah, R. Madsen, W. Sullivan, A. Swidler, and S. Tipton, *Habits of the Heart: Individualism and Commitment in American Life* (Berkeley: University of California Press, 1985). Striking negative comments were made by A. Greeley in his review in *Sociology and Social Research* 70 (1985), as was noticed by S. Lieberson, "Einstein, Renoir, and Greeley: Evidence in Sociology," *American Sociological Review* 57 (1992).

deed, even today, though class distinctions are no more, the jealousies and antipathies they caused have not died out.[29]

In other words, once trust has gone—as anyone who has experienced divorce will surely know—it can never be restored. In this context, it is worth noting that Tocqueville's passionate love of liberty did not prevent him from reaching conclusions that were quite repulsive to him:

> The segregation of classes, which was the crime of the late monarchy, became at a late stage a justification for it, since when the wealthy and enlightened elements of the population were no longer able to act in concert and to take part in the government, the country became, to all intents and purposes, incapable of administering itself and it was needful that a master should step in.[30]

In this there is grandeur. Tocqueville has sufficient stature as a thinker to be able not to write his hopes into history: on the contrary, his hopes pointed one way while his analysis of social and political processes often indicated another. If one hopes that his pessimism may be refuted by contemporary transitions from authoritarianism, his work does at least allow one to be armed so as to confront likely dangers.

But if chances for reform exist, the spirit and legacy of Tocqueville would certainly not seek to secure them by

[29] Tocqueville, *The Old Regime and the French Revolution*, 107.
[30] Ibid.

means of restriction and control. Most immediately, let us remember that Tocqueville liked active independence, contention rather than the dead hand of order and uniformity. At a deeper level, his injunction is always to trust the people: the only guarantee of liberty consists in the hearts of those who know the value of liberty, and that can only be created as the result of living in freedom. The sole way to deal with a decided lack of trust is to persevere in repairing democratic deficits. In the long run, liberty will teach people trust. It is therefore appropriate to conclude with the words of Sting, an English pop star who understands Tocqueville better than does Bellah when proclaiming that "if you love someone, set them free."

CHAPTER 10

Imperialism, the Perversion of Nationalism

John Hobson's celebrated *Imperialism: A Study* begins with striking thoughts about the relationships between nationalism and imperialism.

> The novelty of the recent Imperialism regarded as a policy consists chiefly in its adoption by several nations. The notion of a number of competing empires is essentially modern. The root idea of empire in the ancient and medieval world was that of a federation of States, under a hegemony, covering in general terms the entire or recognized world, such as was held by Rome.... Thus empire was identified with internationalism, though not always based on a conception of equality of nations ... the triumph of nationalism seems to have crushed the rising hope of internationalism. Yet it would appear that there is no essential antagonism between them. A true strong internationalism in form or spirit would rather imply the existence of powerful self-respecting nationalities which seek union on the basis of common national needs and interests.... Nationalism is a plain highway to internationalism, and if it manifests divergence we may well

suspect a perversion of its nature and its purpose. Such a perversion is Imperialism, in which nations trespassing beyond the limits of facile assimilation transform the wholesome stimulative rivalry of varied national types into the cut-throat struggle of competing empires.[1]

There is much to praise here. The ideal typical empire, especially in premodern circumstances, sought to create a world all of its own, free from competitors.[2] Such empires were "multicultural" (perhaps at times even "multinational") to a fault, bound to diversity by weakness, lacking means to indoctrinate and to homogenize into a single mold. Nationalism and imperialism were separated from each other, making any notion of intimacy between them ridiculous. "Recent" imperialism was indeed different, seeking, in different degrees, to homogenize different peoples into a singular identity. These empires sought to become national states.

The main interpretation of the world in which such attempts took place is simple: namely, that nationalism was too powerful a force to allow this. Stated otherwise, nationalism is seen as the force that destroyed empire.[3] It is easy to

---

[1] J. A. Hobson, *Imperialism: A Study* (London, 1902), 6–7, 8. The importance of these pages has been brought to general attention by K. Kumar, "Nation-states as Empires, Empires as Nation-states: Two Principles, One Practice?," *Theory and Society* 39 (2010).

[2] At particular times the universalism of both Chinese and Mughal empires was diluted in practice by the recognition of rivals.

[3] K. J. Holsti, *Peace and War: Armed Conflicts and International Order, 1648–1989* (Cambridge: Cambridge University Press, 1991); S. Van Evera, "Hypotheses on Nationalism and War," *International Security* 18 (1994); B. Miller, *States, Nations and the Great Powers: The Sources of Regional War and Peace* (Cam-

see why. If nationalism means that a nation needs to be protected by its own state, then both irredentism and secession follow logically. Beyond that stands a vicious dynamic: if a state feels that a minority might become a fifth column calling in the state of its external homeland, then preemptive cleansing is called for, something that makes logical early actions on the part of the external homeland in question to protect that minority—a game of mirrors likely to escalate tension.[4] But skepticism is called for here. For one thing, we have already seen that it is at least possible for several nations to live under a political roof, and one can add to this that home rule for Ireland was nearly achieved before 1914, with the Hapsburgs having achieved still more by means of the Moravian Compromise—a development that looked as if it might be applied more generally in the empire. Therefore, secession is not inevitable. For another, recent research has noted the presence of "imperial ethnicities" whose very being focused on loyalty to empire, from varied mixtures of loyalty, belief, and fear—as is obvious once we think of the role of army officers, socialists, and Jews in the Hapsburg empire.[5] But the key generalization is simply that no multi-

bridge: Cambridge University Press, 2007); A. Wimmer and B. Min, "From Empire to Nation-State: Explaining Wars in the Modern World, 1816–2001," *American Sociological Review* 71 (2006); and W. Hiers and A. Wimmer, "Is Nationalism the Cause or Consequence of the End of Empire?," in *Nationalism and War*, ed. J. A. Hall and S. Malešević (Cambridge: Cambridge University Press, forthcoming). I am indebted to Andreas Wimmer (whose work subtly differs from that of the other scholars mentioned here) for comments, and remain in debate with his important work.

[4] M. Mann, *The Dark Side of Democracy: Explaining Ethnic Cleansing* (Cambridge: Cambridge University Press, 2005).

[5] J. Darwin, "Empire and Ethnicity," *Nations and Nationalism* 16 (2010).

national empire was able to turn itself into some sort of nonimperial, modern, liberal political entity. This chapter seeks to explain this failure. Truth to the historical record requires that the answer be complex, involving nationalism and geopolitics, with particular reference to the interaction between these forces.

We can begin by noting that there were two types of empire extant at the end of the nineteenth century: traditional agrarian polities and overseas trading states—that is, empires within Europe itself, as well as the newer ones overseas.[6] The empires of the Romanovs and the Hapsburgs clearly belong to the former "composite" type, having benefited from expansion as the result of conquest, colonization, and marriage. If Britain was the prime example of the latter, it contained the Irish, and so had at least one composite element of its own. It is of the essence of the matter that it was impossible to wholly separate these two forms of empire, although some clearheaded attempts were made to do so. The power of overseas empire could make Continental imperial powers feel insignificant.

In the contemporary world, political economy success derives from intensity, from the benign workings of human capital described by Adam Smith. Presently, brains matter more than the possession of extensive territory, but this is not how things appeared at the end of the nineteenth century. Size was then held to be the means to power, and hence to security. The awful example that proved the point to the

[6] D. Lieven, "Dilemmas of Empire, 1850–1918: Power, Territory, Identity," *Journal of Contemporary History* 34 (1999) and *Empire: The Russian Empire and Its Rivals* (London: John Murray, 2000). I am deeply indebted to Lieven's work.

leading powers was the slow decline of the Ottomans. Millions of Muslims had been driven from the Balkans by 1914, the first massive piece of ethnic cleansing in the industrial era, while the state was totally humiliated in a thousand ways—with its fiscal capacity farmed out to foreigners and its Greek trading elite only too willing to call in support from coreligionists abroad. The "sick man of Europe" sought to reinvent himself, but there was no clear indication as to how this could be done. "Ottomanism" never had mass appeal, and the best bet—the creation of a Muslim identity that would draw in the Arab provinces—had little appeal to the Turkish military elite. The prospect of dismemberment loomed large.

The key dilemma that faced the empires of Continental Europe was simple: if size was to be maintained in the circumstances of the time, as it had to be if power was to be preserved, it was necessary to deal with the national question. Homogeneity would lend cohesion and power, not least as it was believed that citizen armies would gain fighting spirit—as seems to have been demonstrated by the Japanese when fighting Russia in 1905. Accordingly, state elites began to interfere with their peoples. There is ambiguity at this point. On occasion, it seems as if the actions of states actually created national movements where none existed before. But I have no desire to deny that some national movements had already been formed, and that "official nationalisms" attempted to control something that they felt might get out of hand.[7] But in either case, the desire to homoge-

---

[7] B. Anderson, *Imagined Communities: Reflections on the Origin and Spread of Nationalism* (London: Verso, 1983), chapter 6.

nize gave nationalist movements a particular character, turning them from cultural affairs of professors toward popular
movements all-too-capable of political agency. A classic instance of the way in which actions by the state resulted in a
change in the character of a preexisting national movement
is provided by the Finns. Until the end of the nineteenth
century, the Finns had been content within the czarist empire; they were largely left to their own devices, blessed with
the liberties that came with the status of an imperial duchy.
Rationalization policies, especially as they affected language,
led a newly politicized nationalist movement to demand secession by the start of the twentieth century.

From our perspective it might seem as if Great Britain
represented the farthest opposite point to the Ottomans on
a range measuring state strength. It ruled over large parts of
the world; balanced its accounts and paid its military, thanks
to the contributions made by India; had at least some hegemonic powers, especially over the sea lanes; and was soon,
during both world wars, able to call on reserves of manpower that did a good deal to bring about victory. Nonetheless, the British elite felt under threat in structural terms.
The country was, after all, but a small island, yet its possession of so much territory made it something of a freak. The
defeat of the French in the great imperial contest of the late
eighteenth and early nineteenth century had allowed Britain to expand, and the maintenance of its empire resulted
thereafter from, in turn, exhaustion and then balance among
its European rivals.[8] Most of its rule was but skin-deep. Fra-

[8] J. Darwin, *After Tamerlane: The Rise and Fall of Global Empires, 1400–2000*
(Harmondsworth: Penguin, 2007) and *The Empire Project: The Rise and Fall of*

gility also resulted from what is now seen as one of its great
achievements: free trade. Food had to be imported, making
naval supremacy absolutely vital. It was this that made the
German challenge—directed less at the acquisition of colo-
nies than at the capacity to strike at the British fleet—so very
alarming, terrifying far beyond Germany's move toward the
second industrial revolution. But even this understates the
case. Britain was at one with Germany, and with France, in
seeing the future as likely to favor Russia and the United
States, powers with their own continents.

One classic response was articulated by Sir John Seeley in
his demand for a "Greater Britain." It might well be the case
that not everyone could be included in a larger British entity. This certainly applied to Africans, but quite as much to
Indians, even though key early Indian nationalists wanted
to "get in," wanted to be part of a larger Britannic entity. The
empire had racial discrimination at its core, at least in its
later stages, and Seeley's dream was thus for a "Greater Britain" based on the white settlers of Australia, Canada, South
Africa, and New Zealand. There was certainly, as noted, a
measure of shared identity in the white Dominions—and it
led millions to fight for Britain in South Africa as well as in
the world wars. But these plans did not succeed. For one
thing, the settler nations were proud and independent, and
not at all keen to respond to calls for imperial defense, given
their own needs and their increasing frustration at foreign
policy being decided in London. Schemes for a federal empire came to naught, because in the end there was insuffi-

the British World System, 1830–1970 (Cambridge: Cambridge University Press,
2009).

cient interest on either side. And in this context one should remember Ireland. The varied plans for home rule stalemated British politics at the end of the nineteenth century. Indeed, in 1914 Britain faced the possibility of mutiny in its own army, which was reluctant to allow a minority of Protestants to be included in home rule for the entire, largely Catholic island of Ireland and wholly opposed to the setting of a precedent that might lead to a general weakening of the empire.[9] Also, the idea of imperial unity often had tariff reform at its core, that is, the creation of a closed imperial trading bloc. There was powerful resistance to this in Britain itself, for it would likely increase the price of food. Empire might be popular in a vague way, but not when it began to affect the living standards of the people.[10]

Czarist Russia felt equally threatened at the end of the nineteenth century, for all that others felt scared by its sheer size, and especially by its resources of manpower. If German military prowess and industrial power were alarming, so was the alliance with Vienna, since this suggested an alliance between a single people. In these circumstances radical state nationalists sought to enhance Russian power. Industrialization mattered, but so too did the national question. Pure Russian ethnics were, after all, not a majority in the empire. But if Ukrainians could become Russian—that is, if they could be prevented from even creating an identity of their

[9] Lieven nicely notes that democratic pressures made it hard to create federal solutions. Franz Joseph had given great autonomy to the Hungarians in 1867 without consulting anyone; this route was barred in Britain ("Dilemmas of Empire," 197–99).

[10] F. Trentmann, *Free Trade Nation: Consumption, Civil Society and Commerce in Modern Britain* (Oxford: Oxford University Press, 2008).

own—then Russia might have the chance to create at least the core of a nation-state. Extreme harshness thus characterized Russian policy. And we have seen that the prospect of diminished voice raised the attractiveness of exit for the Finns.

The world of Austria-Hungary at once resembled and differed from the Russian situation. Defeat by Germany had led to the granting of autonomy for the Magyars. They were not a majority in their own territory, and so imposed very harsh assimilation conditions—close to success by 1914—on the Slovaks. The Austrian half of the empire, Cisleithenia, was very different. For many years German had simply seemed a world language to which other communities would accede. When this did not happen, when the Czechs started to gain political consciousness, the German community reacted as an ethnic group. But German ethnics were not a majority within Cisleithenia, and certainly nothing like that in the empire as a whole.[11] In these circumstances, the empire moved very slowly to a system of accommodation. This was a world of "bearable dissatisfaction" in the words of Count Taaffe. It is important to remember that no leader of the Czech national movement, to give but one example, sought actual independence during the nineteenth century—with key leaders such as Palacký arguing strongly against such a move, as they were fearful of becoming a

---

[11] German was the language of social mobility, and census returns—always political acts—sought to enhance the number of "Germans" by considering ethnicity in terms of the language in daily use. But even this method—bitterly contested by the Czechs who wanted to enhance their numbers by measuring the "mother tongue"—only produced 38 percent of "Germans" in Cisleithenia, itself, of course, a much smaller percentage for the empire as a whole.

petty state that was all too exposed to German and Russian depredations. The Moravian Compromise looked set to secure loyalty through the granting of cultural rights, and something like this was being planned for the Czechs. But herein lay a major difficulty. The empire really needed a period of peace to consolidate such reforms, all of which were anyway undermining the powers of the central government. But the Hapsburgs wished to continue to play the great game of power politics and were therefore suffering from what can only be termed political schizophrenia; they were forced to accommodate, but in their heart of hearts they were attracted by homogenizing policies that would enhance their geopolitical strength.

Perhaps the best way to characterize what was going on in general terms is by turning to Max Weber, less as a sociologist than as a political actor in his own era. Three points need to be made about the German thinker, two immediately and a third a little later. The first is to recall that Weber's ultimate value was nationalist. The most obvious way in which this can be seen is in his early obsession with the Polish workers in the East Elbian estates of the aristocratic Junker class. National strength would come from homogeneity and cohesion, something that Bismarck had also felt, albeit opportunistically, when opening the cultural wars against the Catholics. Weber recognized that a measure of unity had been achieved through war, but he wished to further German strength in his own time, to achieve something equivalent to the previous generation, which had created the Reich. Any doubt about Weber's nationalist leanings can be seen in his attitude during the First World War, above all, in his concern to extend German power to the East, at the expense of Poland.

The second element of Weber's own politics of concern here is his membership in the Navy League. Weber was representative of many of the statist middle class who believed that Germany deserved and needed its own "place in the sun." Interestingly, his views were criticized by the Austrian marginalists in 1907 when he gave a speech in Vienna on the immediately accurate grounds that the German economy was developing rapidly—able to overtake Great Britain in 1913, according to recent economic historians, without the benefit of much in the way of imperial possessions. However, what matters about economics in the end is, of course, not reality but rather what people believe to be the case. And in this matter there was a measure of rationality to Weber's view. The British turn to free trade and interdependence was, in fact, no such thing: food supplies might come from abroad, but the power of the Royal Navy in effect made Britain autonomous. If a Continental power took the same course, it would be much more dangerous. This is exactly what happened to Germany in the last years of the First World War, when the British blockade bit seriously. As it happens, we now know that this had been planned in London at exactly the time that Weber was being criticized in Vienna.[12]

It is as well to highlight what is involved. By the end of the nineteenth century, European territory was, so to speak, filled, allowing no further expansion on the Continent. In

[12] A. Offer, *The First World War: An Agrarian Interpretation* (Oxford: Clarendon Press, 1989).

these circumstances war would necessarily be a disaster. But the intensity of geopolitical competition, the enormous insecurities of the great powers, meant that the desire for complete autonomy was rampant. One cause of international tensions at the end of the nineteenth century lay in international trade rivalries resulting from dumping practices—themselves the result of every state determining to be autonomous in the production of steel, the base for military independence.[13] But the picture as a whole is best characterized as the marriage of nationalism and imperialism. Each state sought secure sources of supply and secure markets for goods produced. At any particular moment in time this might seem silly, given that the British empire traded openly before 1914. But that could change, as was obvious to those on the Continent who were looking at British politicians from both parties talking about the need for imperial union.

It is time to analyze the manner in which the dilemmas noted played out in practice. Two points will be made, the first a caution, the second drawing a distinction between the character of the two world wars. The caution is simple. It is not the case that the struggle for possessions overseas led immediately to the First World War. Lenin was wrong. Timing disproves his theory: the division of Africa took place in the 1880s. What always mattered most to these great powers was their security within the European heartland—and, more particularly, the determination not to let matters so escalate that anything like the strains and stresses

[13] G. Sen, *The Military Origins of Industrialization and International Trade Rivalry* (London: Frances Pinter, 1984).

of the revolutionary and Napoleonic period be repeated.[14] It was this background condition that made it relatively easy to settle imperial disputes, especially over the partition of Africa. After all, imperial possessions paid little—with the exception of India, which, as noted, mattered enormously for Britain. The balance within Europe is the factor that allowed Britain to gain a huge empire in the first place; equally, geopolitical factors do most to explain its longevity—French resentments were never likely to lead to war, given the increasing power of Germany, while Germany itself for a long time did not wish to increase French and Russian power at the expense of Britain, since that would weaken its own position.[15] Besides, the British empire was, until the interwar period, open to trade from its rivals. In summary, imperial disputes before 1914 were always kept within bounds; they certainly did not actually cause the onset of disaster. Nonetheless, Germany clearly felt left out, as noted, and received the merest trifles despite an activist foreign policy under Kaiser Wilhelm II.

While full agreement as to the origins of the First World War will never be achieved, some comments relating to the argument can be made. Nationalism most certainly played some part in the origin of the war. Most immediately, the occasion for war were the shots fired by the Serbian nationalist Gavrilo Princip, an irredentist nationalist keen to establish a Greater Serbia. More generally, there were traces of the marriage of nationalism and imperialism, not just

[14] Darwin, *After Tamerlane*, 225–26.
[15] P. Kennedy, "Why Did the British Empire Last So Long?," in his *Strategy and Diplomacy, 1870–1945* (London: George Allen and Unwin, 1983).

in an intellectual like Max Weber but also in the mind of Bethmann-Hollweg. Still more important were the feelings in Vienna. The stiff note sent to Serbia, and backed by Germany, was in part caused by the fear that the empire would not be able to compete in a world in which size and national homogeneity mattered so much if it could not control its own territory—that is, if secession by the southern Slavs meant that its power would be undermined, as had been true of that of the Ottomans. Still, the war also had the character of a normal interstate conflict within a multipolar system. As Darwin noted, "the July Crisis revealed that the Achilles' heel of Europe's global primacy was the underdevelopment of the European states system."[16] This draws our attention to the two basic factors, already noted, that tend to explain escalation to the extremes in a system of states. The first is that of heterogeneity in the system as a whole, the presence of different values making mutual understanding difficult. This was certainly present by 1914 in a way that it had not been when Bismarck and Lord Salisbury were conducting the foreign policies of their respective countries. The second is that of the character of the states involved, that is, establishing whether they had the capacity—so often presumed by realism to exist—to calculate rationally. There were clear deficiencies at the time. While the British state had brilliantly retrenched so as to face Germany, domestic politics made it impossible to give Germany the clear warning, by means of an open alliance, that might have prevented conflict. The Hapsburg case was made endlessly difficult by

---

[16] Darwin, *After Tamerlane*, 373.

Hungarian autonomy. But the key variable involved was the inability of the German state to calculate rationally. Middle-class nationalists such as Weber were pressing their state for a more activist policy. But the crucial factor was that the state was really a court, with policy determined by whoever had last gained the ear of the kaiser, and with no priority set between a world policy directed against England and the traditional Eastern policy directed against Russia.[17] The famous 1907 Foreign Office "Memorandum of the Present State of British Relations with France and Germany" written by Eyre Crowe admitted that this explained German behavior as well as any purportedly conscious, aggressive policy:

> It might be suggested that the great German design is in reality no more than the expression of a vague, confused, and unpractical statesmanship, not fully realizing its own drift. A charitable critic might add, by way of explanation, that the well-known qualities of mind and temperament distinguishing for good or for evil the present Ruler of Germany may not improbably be largely responsible for the erratic, domineering, and often frankly aggressive spirit which is recognizable at present in every branch of German public life ... and that this spirit has called forth those manifestations of discontent and alarm both at home and abroad with

---

[17] I. Hull, *The Entourage of Kaiser Wilhelm II, 1888–1918* (Cambridge: Cambridge University Press, 1982); M. Mann, *The Sources of Social Power*, vol. 2, *The Rise of Classes and Nation-States, 1760–1914* (Cambridge: Cambridge University Press, 1993), chapter 21.

which the world is becoming familiar; that, in fact, Germany does not really know what she is driving at, and that all her excursions and alarums, all her underhand intrigues do not contribute to the steady working out of a well-conceived and relentlessly followed system of policy, because they do not really form part of any such system.[18]

And this is where the third point about Weber can be made: he realized precisely this during the war as the result of the idiotic decision to let loose submarines on American shipping. Without this, Germany might have been able to establish hegemony on the Continent.

Industry applied to war, together with the need of a conscription war to have grand aims ("a war to end all wars," "a war for democracy," the promise of "a land fit for heroes"), meant that conflict escalated so as to make it savagely destructive and, with the benefit of hindsight, no longer a rational policy for the states concerned.[19] As institutions were destroyed, everything changed. One crucial consequence was the creation of a whole slew of new nation-states in Central Europe, most of them feeble and in conflict with one another, and many of them with nationalities problems of their own. It is worth highlighting what is involved here. I

[18] E. Crowe, "Memorandum on the Present State of British Relations with France and Germany" (January 1, 1907), in *British Documents on the Origins of the War, 1898–1914*, vol. 3, *The Testing of the Entente, 1904–6*, ed. G. P. Gooch and H. Temperley (London: H. M. Stationery Office, 1928), 415.

[19] It is important to note this here. Sometimes nationalism is blamed for the viciousness of modern wars. There is truth to that, but one needs to remember that increased killing was also the result of technological advance.

began by noting a challenge to traditional theory—namely, the insistence that nationalism was a major cause of war in modern times. This is not quite right.[20] The cause of the war was, as argued, in part traditional. But two other factors need to be stressed. First, it took defeat in war to allow nation-states to emerge. The caging of nations becomes impossible, at this and other times, only when states are thrown into disarray, characteristically by defeat in war. Second, the nationalist movements that then took over had gained political consciousness because of the way in which states had treated them—with Masaryk becoming certain of the need for full independence only very late, and in part in response to the new emperor's plan to "Germanify" Cisleithenia after all. In a nutshell, nationalism mattered, of course, but it has largely been created by the actions of states that were driven to unify their territories in the belief that this was the only way to protect their power. In other words, but for the intensity of geopolitical competition, it is at least possible that the nationalities problem in some places, above all in Cisleithenia, might have been solved in such a way as to allow for several nations to live under a single but necessarily more liberal political roof.

Central Europe then became a power vacuum into which larger states were always likely to be drawn. Crucially, the states involved suffered from social revolutions. The empire to the East had been recreated under new management, a significant part of it Jewish in background, as figures of this sort found that national liberation meant their eventual ex-

---

[20] The key theorist involved now admits this. A. Wimmer and Y. Feinstein, "The Rise of the Nation-State across the World, 1816–2001," *American Sociological Review* 75 (2010).

clusion, so turning them into left-wing empire savers—another example of the impact of nationalism, caused in turn by prior state actions.[21] The Nazi revolution came later, but its foreign policy proved to be still more radical. All this made it impossible to create a sustainable geopolitical settlement in the interwar period. These conditions further played their part in the onset of the Great Depression, and the consequent increasing salience of the politics of economic autarchy. But if protectionism increased international disorder, as Cordell Hull believed, it is as well to remember that it was itself caused by a failure to create order in the world polity.

It was in these circumstances that the marriage of nationalism and imperialism became increasingly important. One element that went into the mix in Germany by 1918 was the experience of food shortages because of the British blockade. Hitler certainly insisted that the possession of territory was a logical necessity. His policy was aggressive and imperial, and it made the Second World War utterly different in character from the First—an interimperial war rather than a traditional conflict in which, at the start, every state claimed war was necessary for defense and protection rather than for expansion. But one cannot leave the matter at this point, for to do so would be to miss the novelty involved. The uniqueness of the German situation was the desire for lebensraum, for an expansion within Europe that would not create, as had traditionally been the case, a multinational polity but rather kill and cleanse so that new territories would be inhabited only by Aryans in the end. The ultimate perversion

---

[21] L. Riga, "The Ethnic Roots of Class Universalism: Rethinking the 'Russian' Revolution," *American Journal of Sociology* 114 (2008).

of nationalism was the polity envisaged by Hitler, in which extermination of difference would allow extension of a single "race."[22]

Some final reflections about the contemporary world polity may help highlight the case that has been made. Two background conditions need to be borne in mind. The first is completely clear. The nuclear revolution is a true global change whose logic—the impossibility in rational terms of using this revolutionary means of destruction—has so far been generally observed. The second change is as important. The Second World War ended European empires. Nationalist (or, better, anti-imperial) militancy made empire too expensive to maintain, especially as European states slowly discovered that they could prosper without overseas territorial control. The crucial argument was made with characteristic lucidity by Raymond Aron.[23] If metropolitan France wished to live up to its promise to make real citizens in all its territorial possessions—blessed by high standards of education, health, and welfare—it would have to face a severe decline in its own living standards. It was not surprising to see that Paris let Algeria go so as to enjoy the standard of living to which it had become accustomed. The logic here has already been noted: power no longer comes from the possession of territory. Of course, not every leader, not least those in Moscow and Beijing, recognizes this.

Two political developments are based on these back-

---

[22] M. Mazower, *Hitler's Empire: How the Nazis Ruled Europe* (New York: Penguin, 2008); S. Baranowksi, *Nazi Empire: German Colonialism from Bismarck to Hitler* (Cambridge: Cambridge University Press, 2011).

[23] R. Aron, *La tragédie Algeriénne* (Paris: Plon, 1957).

ground conditions. Europeans have, in ways that have been stressed, found ways to reconstruct civilities within their world, at least in part due to the manner in which their security problems have been solved by the American presence. Far more impressive than Europe is the wonderful fact that crucial parts of the world have found a route to the modern world that does not involve copying the disasters of the European past. One can at least hope that the strict version of the nation-state—each state with its own culture, each culture with its own state—may be avoided. Design may help. Much more important is the diminution in the intensity of great power rivalry, and especially of its involvement in much of the rest of the world. Relative geopolitical calm may allow states to manage their nations in a less unitary and homogeneous manner. None of this is to deny that many millions have been killed in the putatively peaceful postwar world in civil wars that are very often fueled by ethnic strife—the end result in large part of European colonialism. But there are reasons to hope here, reasons to think that links between nationalism and war may weaken—and this beyond the current diminution in the numbers of such conflicts.

In contrast, there is much to be said for worrying about the situation in China, where the alternative route is being taken—of homogenization through forcible assimilation and the diluting of minority populations by the traditional method of moving in large numbers of the majority population. One worry is that this route may breed violent response, the desire for secession that was present in key parts of Europe in modern times, above all in Tibet, Hong Kong, and

Taiwan. One can note in this regard that the situation in China is in fact rather different from some of the cases noted above. Han Chinese are a massive majority, and it may well be that over time they will have their way; homogenization may yet work. A second worry is greater. There is a sense in which contemporary China resembles Wilhelmine Germany. The regime lacks legitimacy, and it may yet seek it by playing the nationalist card. Certainly new middle-class elements exist; above all, the massive student population that wishes for a more aggressive policy on the part of their state and believe in its right to a central place in world affairs. Eyre Crowe's famous memorandum suggested that Germany, for whatever reasons, wished to break up the British empire so as to supplant it. Interestingly, this view was opposed by Thomas Sanderson on February 21, 1907, in a memorandum in which he saw Germany as "a helpful, though somewhat exacting friend," adding that "it is altogether contrary to reason that Germany should wish to quarrel with us." Sir Charles Hardinge sent this memorandum to the foreign secretary a few days later on February 25, noting that "somewhat to my surprise he has taken up the cudgels for Germany."[24] It is absolutely true that Germany was prospering in 1914 within the rules of the world order of the time, and looked set to prosper much more. The same is true of China today. One hopes that the result of developments in the two countries will differ, with Chinese behavior to this point justifying worry rather than fear.

[24] T. Sanderson, "Memorandum," in *British Documents*, ed. Gooch and Temperley, 430, 431, and 420, and 420–33 passim.

Conclusion

The main tenets of the argument are clear. Anxiety and even hostility have been shown to the actions of states; when they put ideological dreams into effect, they become enemies of civility, and all too often politicize social actors so as to make them recalcitrant. Virtue should not be the business of states, and visions should remain private, the stuff of nightmares best forgotten when waking. This is not to say for a moment that states are not needed. Civil behavior by political elites can lead to the creation and maintenance of an inclusive and open frame within which people, blessed with negative resisting power, can experiment with their lives. Oscar Wilde was right to insist that "selfishness is not living as one wishes to live, it is asking others to live as one wishes to live."[1] Total moral unity is perhaps always impossible, and certainly so in complex societies. People are all over the place, and sex is ridiculous whichever way you do it. Accordingly, skepticism has been shown to communitarian visions, and the world of civility has been embraced because the obduracy and deviousness of our passions gives us quite enough drama within it. But no social theory is perfect, and it is well to admit that there are tensions within this one. For one thing, the insistence on trusting the people sits uneasily

[1] O. Wilde, "The Soul of Man under Socialism," in *De Profundis and Other Writings* ([1891] London: Penguin, 1973), 49.

with the rather passive role accorded to popular politics. For another, there is a virtual contradiction when discussing state behavior. This has been and can be the source of disaster, but this has not stopped me from seeking for an increase in the intelligence of states. Some hopes can be entertained in this regard: a diminution in the intensity of geopolitical rivalry can allow states to be less unitary; elites may realize that decompression can serve their own interests; and the demands of a changing international political economy may encourage elites to adopt policies that support human capital. Still, these tensions remind us that civility is fragile. It was born from stalemate and reconstructed only as the result of geopolitical triumph over its great enemies.

An even greater problem should at least be mentioned. A dull, material background to all that has been said, noted but not truly highlighted, has been the possibility of economic growth—that is, the creation of decent sufficiencies and negative resisting power, together with the ability to paper over many cracks in society by means of an expansion of the total "pie" of society. Powerful voices stand against such dull materialism and stress both moral and logical limits to what can be achieved by growth. The alternatives to growth suggested are, sadly, deeply unconvincing. Fred Hirsch's imaginative call for status and reward to be disconnected omits any consideration of power, of the ability of the rich to maintain their position.[2] Paul Aries's belief that a popular demand for an end to growth is possible seems even

---

[2] F. Hirsch, *Social Limits to Growth* (London: Routledge and Kegan Paul, 1977).

more far-fetched.[3] Within advanced societies, growth remains the currency of electoral politics, making thought about zero growth—which would probably have to be enforced—almost redundant. But it is, of course, the international dimension that makes it impossible to imagine a no-growth system. Suppose that the United Nations decided that there should be no growth at all in the world as a whole. How would this be possible? Developing countries, above all China, would not accept that advanced societies continue to maintain their industrial machines if that was to limit them to lower standards in perpetuity, and it is again enough to ask whether advanced countries would voluntarily give up some of their standard of living to the South to know the answer. Bluntly, the demand for growth will not cease, with all that this means for global warming. At worst, in such circumstances, the size of states—the ability to have secure sources of supply and secure markets—may once again begin to matter, with all the dangers that such a development would bring to world politics, as well as to the environment. At best, catastrophe—for example, the flooding of populous, low-lying states, with consequent massive migration—might lead to international coordinating policies.[4] Basic honesty requires highlighting my own position. Growth is not just unavoidable but also desirable. Coordination of policy and a forceful move to alternative energy

[3] P. Aries, *La simplicité contre le mythe de l'abondance* (Paris: La Découverte, 2011).

[4] T. Homer-Dixon, *The Upside of Down: Catastrophe, Creativity and the Renewal of Civilization* (Washington, D.C.: Island Press, 2006).

sources can diminish the strain on the planet. But it would be naive not to admit that I place hope and faith in the inventive capacities of science and technology to provide new sources of energy. If the future of civility depends on such development, the route to its achievement looks to be horrifyingly difficult.

The idea that shock can bring us to our senses is present in Immanuel Kant's wonderful essay on perpetual peace. It is often forgotten that he went so far as to say, with regret, that war remained necessary: the horrors of war would create the discipline needed to ensure that we appreciated the benefits of peace.[5] The horrors of the twentieth century reminded us of the benefits of civility. But one wonders how long this historical lesson can last. There is an elective affinity between the position advocated in this book and that of Adam Smith. His advocacy of the benefits of wealth has, as noted, received substantial empirical support.[6] Still more important surely is the superlative sociological understanding of the cohesion brought about by the endless competitive emulation at the heart of modern society. But there is also a significant difference. His friend Dugald Stewart recorded one of his basic presuppositions.

It was the general diffusion of wealth among the lower orders of men, which first gave birth to the spirit of

[5] I. Kant, *Perpetual Peace: A Philosophical Sketch*, in *Kant: Political Writings*, ed. H. Reiss, trans. H. B. Nisbet ([1795] Cambridge: Cambridge University Press, 1971).
[6] B. Friedman, *The Moral Consequences of Economic Growth* (New York: Alfred A. Knopf, 2005).

independence in modern Europe, and which has produced under some of its governments, and especially
under our own, a more equal diffusion of freedom and
of happiness than took place under the most celebrated constitutions of antiquity.[7]

This is very much a part of his general sympathy for labor.
He was an eighteenth-century thinker, aware of rank but
nonetheless insistent that all human beings counted and deserved protection and nurture. One problem with this view
concerns nationalism, the tendency of modern societies to
so limit their citizenship rules as to be inhospitable to immigrants. It is very noticeable in this regard that an advanced social democracy such as Denmark has enormous
difficulty, both in welcoming those that its low birth rate
necessitates and then including them within society, above
all through intermarriage with native Danes. For all its
faults, the United States has a much prouder record in this
regard. A second problem is that of the massive increase in
inequality both in incomes and in wealth. This development is particularly marked in the United States, but it is
present in most other Anglo-Saxon countries as well. This is
utterly opposed to the very nature of civility, which rests
firmly on the presence of sufficient means for self-expression, as well as the ability to resist arbitrary subordination.
Furthermore, in the long run such polarization is likely to
undermine the levels of human capital upon which progress
within capitalist society has depended. The paradoxical

[7] D. Stewart, "An Account of the Life and Writings of Adam Smith, LL.D.," in
A. Smith, *Writings on Philosophical Subjects*, 313.

weakness in the position advocated here should once again be admitted. Social life can run according to its own rhythm when states do not interfere with their societies. But there are limits to this essentially passive view. Social life needs that "general diffusion" of sufficiency to make life meaningful. When the depredations of the rich undermine that, there is clearly a need for struggle, for a more active view of democratic life. But this can be hard to find, given, for example, the role of money in the American electoral process. And there are further worrying developments with capitalist society. At the end of the Second World War, Keynes argued for creating stability in the international economy by mechanisms designed to regulate the behavior both of indebted and creditor countries. The power of the United States at the time led them to reject a plan that would have diminished their position, though with hindsight the leaders of the great superpower may now regret this. But the point is that imbalances in the contemporary world economy, in which finance plays such a massive role, are causing chaos, both within Europe and the larger world. Huge savings must go somewhere, and they are all too likely to be lent out in such a way as to lower interest rates in the receiving countries, thereby causing bubbles of one sort or another that are capable at times of threatening genuine depression. There are enormous complexities here—the desirability of the United States living within its means and of the Chinese changing their pattern of development so as to use savings at home—but there is no reason to believe that we are doomed to disaster. Nonetheless, at times it does seem as if Kant's insistence that discipline can only be recreated by the experience of disaster may well be all too true.

The focus of this book has deliberately been on the core of the advanced world in order to gain a firm understanding of the nature of civility. But the most appropriate way to end this book is to set the extension of civility within the rest of the world against the worries noted. Heady hopes have been raised by the Arab Spring, not least since it initially seemed that these societies were stalemated in a way familiar from the European past. However, in key countries the power of established elites remains, with opposition most likely to come from Islamist groups, whose radicalism could easily increase if they are treated badly by those elites. Additionally, the situation of Arab countries differs hugely from that of the erstwhile communist countries: entry into Europe is not an option. It may well be that Turkey can show a way forward, for here the tensions between the deep state and a religious society look set to be managed successfully—making it all the more stupid of the European Union to exclude its neighbor. So much is to be done here if hopes are to be realized. The fabulous economic success of modern China, in contrast, looks secure: enormous numbers have been raised out of poverty, and sufficient means have been created to allow, happily, for a more contentious society. The loss of legitimacy of the Communist Party may lead to a rise of aggressive nationalism, but a softer political landing is more likely, given the restraints imposed both by nuclear weapons and by the nature of the international economy. And it is likely that China has the capacity to create a homogencous nation-state, unpleasant though it is to admit this. But parts of the developing world have managed their nationalities problem by political arrangements that allow several nations to live under a single political roof in an entirely novel and wholly progressive manner. The achievement of India is totally marvelous in this regard, and the practices involved have reached elsewhere, in parts of Africa and in Indonesia. A diminution of geopolitical conflict may, as noted, allow states to continue to be less unitary. This is not to ignore terrible problems—the presence of weak states, the caging of Indians by caste, the presence of civil war, and the obvious occasions on which nationally homogenizing polices have been tried to disastrous effect. But if hope here must be mixed with fear, it is remarkable that hopes can now be entertained at all. And there can be no doubt about the complete success of many postcommunist societies, above all, those of the Baltics and Central Europe but with marked improvements even in the Balkans. For anyone who knew actually existing communism in its last years, this development is well-nigh miraculous. All in all, faltering in the core of the advanced world is massively outweighed by the remarkable and unexpected spread of civility in the rest of the world.

INDEX

19; religion in, 217; taxation in,
215, 217–18
France Libre, La, 106
Frankfurt School, 165, 171
Frederick the Great, 119
freedom: and the aristocracy, 204–5;
and commercial society, 35, 49; in
England, 212–13, 220–21; and
equality, 205–6, 210–16; in Europe, 211–21; in France, 212–19;
and religion, 208–10; and the self,
132–35, 141; and socialism, 183;
and trust, 202, 215–16, 225; in the
United States, 205–11
free trade, 232, 233
French Revolution, 35, 88, 216
Freud, Sigmund, 12, 85, 172, 183, 218;
Moses and Monotheism, 98–99

Gellner, Ernest, 67–68, 83–85, 86,
91, 129, 172–73, 191–92
Genealogy of Morals (Nietzsche), 1
Germany, 232, 234; class relations in,
113; in the First World War, 236,
239–43, 246; Nazism, 147, 243;
radicalism in, 64, 65–66, 74, 79–
80; Weimar Republic, 19–20, 81
Gibbon, Edward, 32
Giddens, Anthony: *Capitalism and
Modern Social Theory*, 8–9
global warming, 249
Goebbels, Joseph, 159–60
Goffman, Erving, 130–32, 134, 135–
47, 150–51; *Asylums*, 136, 141,
145; *The Presentation of the Self in*

Everyday Life, 130; *Relations in
Public*, 144–45; "Role Distance,"
142; *Stigma*, 146–47
Gompers, Samuel, 64
Goodwin, Jeff: *No Other Way Out*,
72, 73
Gorbachev, Mikhail, 192–93,
198–200
Gouldner, Alvin: *The Coming Crisis
of Western Sociology*, 130–31
Gramsci, Antonio, 165
Grande Schisme, Le (Aron), 111
Grass, Günter, 148n30
Great Debate, The (Aron), 111
Greece, 101
Griffith, D. W., 159

Habermas, Jürgen, 153, 174
habit, 144
Habits of the Heart (Bellah et al.),
223
Halévy, Élie, 183, 221
happiness, 53–54
Hapsburg Empire, 69, 228, 229, 235,
239–40
Hardinge, Charles, 246
Havel, Václav, 73
Heidegger, Martin, 152, 159
Henderson, Arthur, 64
heroism, 188, 189
Hirsch, Fred, 248
Hirschman, Albert: *Exit, Voice and
Loyalty*, 68
History of the Russian Revolution
(Trotsky), 64

Kádár, János, 191
Kafka, Franz, 85
Kant, Immanuel, 250, 252–53
Kavadh I, 187
Keynes, Maynard, 14, 38–39, 158, 252
Kierkegaard, Søren, 176

labor: Adam Smith's sympathy with, 44–45, 251; division of, 40, 41–42, 58. *See also* human capital
Labour Party, 64, 65
Laitin, David, 76–77
language policy: in Cisleithenia, 234n11; in France, 169–70; in India, 77–78, 103; in Ukraine, 102–3; in the United States, 94–95
Languedoc, 218–19
law, rule of, 20, 29
Lenin, Vladimir, 237; *What Is to Be Done?*, 66
liberal democracy, 74–76, 91
liberalism, 2, 10, 67, 75, 90, 91, 99
liberalization, 190–200, 223
liberty. *See* freedom
Libya, 173
Lincoln, Abraham, 94
Lipset, Seymour Martin, 93
literature, sociology of, 168–71
Lonely Crowd, The (Riesman), 52, 131, 148, 149
Louis XIV, 213
Louis XVI, 198
love, 42
Lukács, Georg, 165

Machiavelli, Niccolò, 62–63, 112; *The Discourses*, 62, 81; *The Prince*, 1, 2, 62, 67
macroforces, 7
mafiosi, 20
Mandeville, Bernard, 42, 56
Mann, Michael, 81, 124
Marcuse, Herbert, 165
Mare au Diable, La (Sand), 169
market principle, 40, 41–42
Marx, Karl, 8, 11, 20, 30, 57, 63–65, 85, 176–79, 183, 184
Marxism, 165, 170
Masaryk, Tomáš, 69, 83, 242
masks. *See* roles
Matthys, Jan, 185
mercantilism, 60
microbehavior, 7
military service, 58
Mill, John Stuart, 91
Miller, David, 91
Mills, C. Wright, 8
Misanthrope, The (Molière), 129
misery, 152–53, 154–57
modernism, 162–63, 171–73
modernity, 152–53
Molière: *The Misanthrope*, 129
monasticism, 186, 187, 188
moneymaking, 23, 38–39. *See also* commercial society
Montesquieu, 10–11, 12, 31, 38, 105, 108, 188, 204; *Considerations on the Grandeur and Decadence of the Romans*, 23; *The Persian Letters*, 23–26; *The Spirit of the Laws*, 23
morality, 2–4, 62–63. *See also* virtue
Moravian Compromise, 228, 235

Taaffe, Count, 234
Taborites, 185
Taff Vale, 65
Taiwan, 246
Tanzania, 104
taxation, 215, 217–18, 219–20
Taylor, Charles, 12
Thatcher, Margaret, 71–72
Theory of Moral Sentiments, The
(Smith), 50–56
Thirty Years' War, 30, 75
Thoreau, Henry David, 156
Thucydides, 112
Tibet, 245
Tocqueville, Alexis de, 80, 81, 140,
158, 159, 196, 198, 200, 201–25;
Democracy in America, 205–11;
*The Old Regime and the French
Revolution*, 211, 212–18; on the
United States, 205–11
toleration: in agrarian civilizations,
26–27; and Indian civilization,
33–34; and Islam, 33; origins of in
Europe, 27–33; and pluralism, 87.
See also difference; diversity
totalitarianism, 189–90, 191, 197
tradition, 84
Trajan, 195
transnationalism, 88n9
Treaty of Augsburg, 30
Trotsky, Leon: *History of the Russian
Revolution*, 64
Truffaut, François, 146
trust, 201–3; and class cooperation,
215, 218–19; and envy, 215–16,
223–24; and freedom, 202, 215–

16, 225; and the state, 208, 213–
14, 222
Turkey, 230, 253

Ukraine, 102–3
Ulysses (Joyce), 171–72
unemployment, 71–72
United States: African Americans, 5,
93, 96, 97; associations in, 80;
civic nationalism in, 88, 92–98,
103; Civil War, 94; Cold War, 111,
113, 122; Constitution, 93, 94,
207; equality in, 205–6, 210–11;
ethnic nationalism in, 96; ethnic
relations in, 95–98; freedom in,
205–11; geography of, 206–7; immigration in, 15, 92, 98, 251; and
the international economy, 252;
Iraq War, 120–21, 123; language
policy in, 94–95; legal system in,
207; political engagement in,
207–8; radicalism in, 64, 65; religion in, 93n16, 208–10; role in
Europe of, 74, 75, 245; socialism
in, 95; Tocqueville on, 205–11;
Vietnam War, 117; welfare in, 98
utilitarianism, 115–16
utility, 52–53

Vendée, La, 88
Vidal, Gore: *Creation*, 26
Vietnam War, 117
violence, organized, 6, 6n8. *See also*
war

virtue, 11, 15, 42–43, 75, 247. *See also* morality

war, 112–25; and civility, 105; definition of, 118–19; First World War, 74, 113, 124, 235–43, 246; Hundred Years' War, 217; and international law, 105, 113–14; Iraq War, 120–21, 123; and nationalism, 7, 74, 242; necessity of, 250; Second World War, 6, 243–44; Vietnam War, 117
Washington, George, 3
wealth, 53–54. *See also* commercial society; moneymaking
Wealth of Nations, The (Smith), 40, 43–46, 47–49, 50, 55, 56, 59–60
Webb, Beatrice, 183, 184
Webb, Sidney, 183, 184
Weber, Max, 8, 31, 62, 79–80, 108, 109, 153, 174–75, 179–83, 186, 187, 235–36, 239, 240, 241

Weimar Republic, 19–20, 81
welfare systems, 91, 98, 102
What Is to Be Done? (Lenin), 66
Wilde, Oscar, 4, 150, 247; "The Soul of Man under Socialism," 4
Wilhelm II, 238
Wilkes, John, 32, 99
Wittgenstein, Ludwig, 152
working classes. *See* class struggle
World War I. *See* First World War
World War II. *See* Second World War

Xenophon, 11

Yeltsin, Boris, 199
Yugoslavia, 76

Zionism, 86
Žižek, Slavoj, 174
Zola, Émile, 170